Contents

CONTINUED

The Call of the Wild

Jack London

Chapter 

Into the Primitive

"Old longings nomadic leap,
Chafing at custom's chain;
Again from its brumal sleep
Wakens the ferine strain."

BUCK DID NOT READ the newspapers, or he would have known that trouble was brewing, not alone for himself, but for every tidewater dog, strong of muscle and with warm, long hair, from Puget Sound to San Diego. Because men, groping in the Arctic darkness, had found a yellow metal, and because steamship and transportation companies were booming the find, thousands of men were rushing into the Northland. These men wanted dogs, and the dogs they wanted were heavy dogs, with strong muscles by which to toil, and furry coats to protect them from the frost.

Buck lived at a big house in the sun-kissed Santa Clara Valley. Judge Miller's place, it was called. It stood back from the road, half hidden among the trees, through which glimpses could be caught of the wide, cool veranda that ran around its four sides. The house was approached by graveled driveways which wound about through wide-spreading lawns and under the interlacing boughs of tall poplars. At the rear things were on even a more spacious scale than at the front. There were great stables, where a dozen grooms and boys held forth, rows of vine-clad servants' cottages, an endless and orderly array of outhouses, long grape arbors, green pastures, orchards, and berry patches. Then there was the pumping plant for the artesian well, and the big cement tank where Judge Miller's boys took their morning plunge and kept cool in the hot afternoon.

And over this great demesne Buck ruled. Here he was born, and here he had lived the four years of his life. It was true, there were other dogs. There could not but be other dogs on so vast a place, but they did not count. They came and went, resided in the populous kennels, or lived obscurely in the recesses of the house after the fashion of Toots, the Japanese pug, or Ysabel, the Mexican hairless—strange creatures that rarely put nose out of doors or set foot to ground. On the other hand, there were the fox terriers, a score of them at least, who yelped fearful promises at Toots and Ysabel looking out of the windows at them and protected by a legion of housemaids armed with brooms and mops.

But Buck was neither house dog nor kennel dog. The whole realm was his. He plunged into the swimming tank or went hunting with the Judge's sons; he escorted Mollie and Alice, the Judge's daughters, on long twilight or early-morning rambles; on wintry nights he lay at the Judge's feet before the roaring library fire; he carried the Judge's grandsons on his back, or rolled them in the grass, and guarded their footsteps through wild adventures down to the fountain in the stable yard, and even beyond, where the paddocks were, and the berry patches. Among the terriers he stalked imperiously, and Toots and Ysabel he utterly ignored, for he was king—king over all creeping, crawling, flying things of Judge Miller's place, humans included.

His father, Elmo, a huge St. Bernard, had been the Judge's inseparable companion, and Buck bid fair to follow in the way of his father. He was not so large—he weighed only one hundred and forty pounds—for his mother, Shep, had been a Scotch shepherd dog. Nevertheless one hundred and forty pounds, to which was added the dignity that comes of good living and universal respect, enabled him to carry himself in right royal fashion. During the four years since his puppyhood he had lived the life of a sated aristocrat; he had a fine pride in himself, was even a trifle egotistical, as country gentlemen sometimes become because of their insular situation. But he had saved himself by not becoming a mere pampered house dog. Hunting and kindred outdoor delights had kept down the fat and hardened his muscles; and to him, as to the coldtubbing races, the love of water had been a tonic and a health preserver.

And this was the manner of dog Buck was in the fall of 1897, when the Klondike strike dragged men from all the world into the frozen North. But Buck did not read the newspapers, and he did not know that Manuel, one of the gardener's helpers, was an undesirable acquaintance. Manuel had one besetting sin. He loved to play Chinese lottery. Also, in his gambling, he had one besetting weakness—faith in a system; and this made his damnation certain. For to play a system requires money, while the wages of a gardener's helper do not lap over the needs of a wife and numerous progeny.

The Judge was at a meeting of the Raisin Growers' Association, and the boys were busy organizing an athletic club, on the memorable night of Manuel's treachery. No one saw him and Buck go off through the orchard on what Buck imagined was merely a stroll. And with the exception of a solitary man, no one saw them arrive at the little flag station known as College Park. This man talked with Manuel, and money chinked between them.

"You might wrap up the goods before you deliver 'm," the stranger said gruffly, and Manuel doubled a piece of stout rope around Buck's neck under the collar.

"Twist it, an' you'll choke 'm plentee," said Manuel, and the stranger grunted a ready affirmative.

Buck had accepted the rope with quiet dignity. To be sure, it was an unwonted performance: but he had learned to trust in men he knew, and to give them credit for a wisdom that outreached his own. But when the ends of the rope were placed in the stranger's hands, he growled menacingly. He had merely intimated his displeasure, in his pride believing that to intimate was to command. But to his surprise the rope tightened around his neck, shutting off his breath. In quick rage he sprang at the man, who met him halfway, grappled him close by the throat, and with a deft twist threw him over on his back. Then the rope tightened mercilessly, while Buck struggled in a fury, his tongue lolling out of his mouth and his great chest panting futilely. Never in all his life had he been so vilely treated, and never in all his life had he been so angry. But his strength ebbed, his eyes glazed, and he knew nothing when the train was flagged and the two men threw him into the baggage car.

The next he knew, he was dimly aware that his tongue was hurting and that he was being jolted along in some kind of a conveyance. The hoarse shriek of a locomotive whistling a crossing told him where he was. He had traveled too often with the Judge not to know the sensation of riding in a baggage car. He opened his eyes, and into them came the unbridled anger of a kidnaped king. The man sprang for his throat, but Buck was too quick for him. His jaws closed on the hand, nor did they relax till his senses were choked out of him once more.

"Yep, has fits," the man said, hiding his mangled hand from the baggageman, who had been attracted by the sounds of struggle. "I'm takin 'm up for the boss to 'Frisco. A crack dog doctor there thinks that he can cure 'm."

Concerning that night's ride, the man spoke most eloquently for himself, in a little shed back of a saloon on the San Francisco waterfront.

"All I get is fifty for it," he grumbled; "an' I wouldn't do it over for a thousand, cold cash."

His hand was wrapped in a bloody handkerchief, and the right trouser leg was ripped from knee to ankle.

"How much did the other mug get?" the salonnkeeper demanded.

"A hundred," was the reply. "Wouldn't take a sou less, so help me."

"That makes a hundred and fifty," the saloonkeeper calculated; "and he's worth it, or I'm a squarehead."

The kidnaper undid the bloody wrappings and looked at his lacerated hand. "If I don't get the hydrophoby—"

It'll be because you was born to hang," laughed the saloonkeeper. "Here, lend me a hand before you pull your freight," he added.

Dazed, suffering intolerable pain from throat and tongue, with the life half throttled out of him, Buck attempted to face his tormentors. But he was thrown down and choked repeatedly, till they succeeded in filing the heavy brass collar from off his neck. Then the rope was removed, and he was flung into a cagelike crate.

There he lay for the remainder of the weary night, nursing his wrath and wounded pride. He could not understand what it all meant. What did they want with him, these strange men? Why were they keeping him pent up in this narrow crate? He did not know why, but he felt oppressed by the vague sense of impending calamity. Several times during the night he sprang to his feet when the shed door rattled open, expecting to see the Judge, or the boys at least. But each time it was the bulging face of the saloonkeeper that peered in at him by the sickly light of a tallow candle. And each time the joyful bark that trembled in Buck's throat was twisted into a savage growl.

But the saloonkeeper let him alone, and in the morning four men entered and picked up the crate. More tormentors, Buck decided, for they were evil-looking creatures, ragged and unkempt; and he stormed and raged at them through the bars. They only laughed and poked sticks at him, which he promptly assailed with his teeth till he realized that that was what they wanted. Whereupon he lay down sullenly and allowed the crate to be lifted into a wagon. Then he, and the crate in which he was imprisoned, began a passage through many hands. Clerks in the express office took charge of him; he was carted about in another wagon; a truck carried him, with an assortment of boxes and parcels, upon a ferry steamer; he was trucked off the steamer into a great railway depot, and finally he was deposited in an express car.

For two days and nights this express car was dragged along at the tail of shrieking locomotives; and for two days and nights Buck neither ate nor drank. In his anger he had met the first advances of the express messsengers with growls, and they had retaliated by teasing him. When he flung himself against the bars, quivering and frothing, they laughed at him and taunted him. They growled and barked like detestable dogs, mewed, and flapped their arms and crowed. It was all very silly, he knew; but therefore the more outrage to his dignity, and his anger waxed and waxed. He did not mind the hunger so much, but the lack of water caused him severe suffering and fanned his wrath to fever pitch. For that matter, high-strung and finely sensitive, the ill treatment had flung him into a fever, which was fed by the inflammation of his parched and swollen throat and tongue.

He was glad for one thing: the rope was off his neck. That had given them an unfair advantage; but now that it was off, he would show them. They would never get another rope around his neck. Upon that he was resolved. For two days and nights he neither ate nor drank, and during those two days and nights of torment, he accumulated a fund of wrath that boded ill for whoever first fell foul of him. His eyes turned bloodshot, and he was metamorphosed into a raging fiend. So changed was he that the Judge himself would not have recognized him; and the express messengers breathed with relief when they bundled him off the train at Seattle.

Four men gingerly carried the crate from the wagon into a small, high-walled back yard. A stout man, with a red sweater that sagged generously at the neck, came out and signed the book for the driver. That was the man, Buck divined, the next tormentor, and he hurled himself savagely against the bars. The man smiled grimly, and brought a hatchet and a club.

"You ain't going to take him out now?" the driver asked.

"Sure," the man replied, driving the hatchet into the crate for a pry.

There was an instantaneous scattering of the four men who had carried it in, and from safe perches on top of the wall they prepared to watch the performance.

Buck rushed at the splintering wood, sinking his teeth into it, surging and wrestling with it. Wherever the hatchet fell on the outside, he was there on the inside, snarling and growling, as furiously anxious to get out as the man in the red sweater was calmly intent on getting him out.

"Now, you red-eyed devil," he said, when he had made an opening sufficient for the passage of Buck's body. At the same time he dropped the hatchet and shifted the club to his right hand.

And Buck was truly a red-eyed devil, as he drew himself together for the spring, hair bristling, mouth foaming, a mad glitter in his bloodshot eyes. Straight at the man he launched his one hundred and forty pounds of fury, surcharged with the pent passion of two days and nights. In midair, just as his jaws were about to close on the man, he received a shock that checked his body and brought his teeth together with an agonizing clip. He whirled over, fetching the ground on his back and side. He had never been struck by a club in his life, and did not understand. With a snarl that was part bark and more scream he was again on his feet and launched into the air. And again the shock came and he was brought crushingly to the ground. This time he was aware that it was the club, but his madness knew no caution. A dozen times he charged, and as often the club broke the charge and smashed him down.

After a particularly fierce blow, he crawled to his feet, too dazed to rush. He staggered limply about, the blood flowing from nose and mouth and ears, his beautiful coat sprayed and flecked with bloody slaver. Then the man advanced and deliberately dealt him a frightful blow on the nose. All the pain he had endured was as nothing compared with the exquisite agony of this. With a roar that was almost lionlike in its ferocity, he again hurled himself at the man. But the man, shifting the club from right to left, coolly caught him by the under jaw, at the same time wrenching downward and backward. Buck described a complete circle in the air, and half of another, then crashed to the ground on his head and chest.

For the last time he rushed. The man struck the shrewd blow he had purposely withheld for so long, and Buck crumpled up and went down, knocked utterly senseless.

"He's no slouch at dog-breakin', that's wot I say," one of the men on the wall cried enthusiastically.

"Druther break cayuses any day, and twice on Sundays," was the reply of the driver, as he climbed on the wagon and started the horses.

Buck's senses came back to him, but not his strength. He lay where he had fallen, and from there he watched the man in the red sweater.

" 'Answers to the name of Buck,' " the man soliloquized, quoting from the saloonkeeper's letter, which had announced the consignment of the crate and contents. "Well, Buck, my boy," he went on in a genial voice, "we've had our little ruction, and the best thing we can do is to let it go at that. You've learned your place, and I know mine. Be a good dog and all'll go well and the goose hang high. Be a bad dog, and I'll whale the stuffin' outa you. Understand?"

As he spoke he fearlessly patted the head he had so mercilessly pounded, and though Buck's hair involuntarily bristled at touch of the hand, he endured it without protest. When the man brought him water he drank eagerly, and later bolted a generous meal of raw meat, chunk by chunk, from the man's hand.

He was beaten (he knew that); but he was not broken. He saw, once for all, that he stood no chance against a man with a club. He had learned the lesson, and in all his after life he never forgot it. That club was a revelation. It was his introduction to the reign of primitive law, and he met the introduction halfway. The facts of life took on a fiercer aspect; and while he faced that aspect uncowed, he faced it with all the latent cunning of his nature aroused. As the days went by, other dogs came, in crates and at the ends of ropes, some docilely, and some raging and roaring as he had come; and, one and all, he watched them pass under the dominion of the man in the red sweater. Again and again, as he looked at each brutal performance, the lesson was driven home to Buck: a man with a club was a lawgiver, a master to be obeyed, though not necessarily conciliated. Of this last Buck was never guilty, though he did see beaten dogs that fawned upon the man, and wagged their tails, and licked his hands. Also he saw one dog, that would neither conciliate nor obey, finally killed in the struggle for mastery.

Now and again men came, strangers, who talked excitedly, wheedlingly and in all kinds of fashions to the man in the red sweater. And at such times that money passed between them the strangers took one or more of the dogs away with them. Buck wondered where they went, for they never came back; but the fear of the future was strong upon him, and he was glad each time when he was not selected.

Yet his time came, in the end, in the form of a little weazened man who spat broken English and many strange and uncouth exclamations which Buck could not understand.

"*Sacrédam!*" he cried, when his eyes lit upon Buck. Dat one dam bully dog! Eh? How moch?"

"Three hundred, and a present at that," was the prompt reply of the man in the red sweater. "And seein' it's government money, you ain't got no kick coming, eh, Perrault?"

Perrault grinned. Considering that the price of dogs had been boomed skyward by the unwonted demand, it was not an unfair sum for so fine an animal. The Canadian Government would be no loser, nor would its dispatches travel the slower. Perrault knew dogs, and when he looked at Buck he knew that he was one in a thousand. "One in ten t'ousand" he commented mentally.

Buck saw money pass between them, and was not surprised when Curly, a good-natured Newfoundland, and he were led away by the little weazened man. That was the last he saw of the man in the red sweater, and as Curly and he looked at receding Seattle from the deck of the *Narwhal,* it was the last he saw of the warm Southland. Curly and he were taken below by Perrault and turned over to a black-faced giant called François. Perrault was a French-Canadian, and swarthy; but François was a French-Canadian half-breed, and twice as swarthy. They were a new kind of men to Buck (of which he was destined to see many more), and while he developed no affection for them, he none the less grew honestly to respect them. He speedily learned that Perrault and François were fair men, calm and impartial in administering justice, and too wise in the way of dogs to be fooled by dogs.

In the 'tween decks of the *Narwhal,* Buck and Curly joined two other dogs. One of them was a big, snow-white fellow from Spitzbergen who had been brought away by a whaling captain, and who had later accompanied a Geological Survey into the Barrens. He was friendly, in a treacherous sort of way, smiling into one's face the while he meditated some underhand trick, as, for instance, when he stole from Buck's food at the first meal. As Buck sprang to punish him, the lash of François's whip sang through the air, reaching the culprit first; and nothing remained to Buck but to recover the bone. That was fair of François, he decided, and the half-breed began his rise in Buck's estimation.

The other dog made no advances, nor received any; also, he did not attempt to steal from the newcomers. He was a gloomy, morose fellow, and he showed Curly plainly that all he desired was to be left alone, and further, that there would be trouble if he were not left alone. Dave he was called, and he ate and slept, or yawned between times, and took interest in nothing, not even when the *Narwhal* crossed Queen Charlotte Sound and rolled and pitched and bucked like a thing possessed. When Buck and Curly grew excited, half wild with fear, he raised his head as though annoyed, favored them with an incurious glance, yawned, and went to sleep again.

Day and night the ship throbbed to the tireless pulse of the propeller, and though one day was very like another, it was apparent to Buck that the weather was steadily growing colder. At last, one morning, the propeller was quiet, and the *Narwhal* was pervaded with an atmosphere of excitement. He felt it, as did the other dogs, and knew that a change was at hand. François leashed them and brought them on deck. At the first step upon the cold surface, Buck's feet sank into a white mushy something very much like mud. He sprang back with a snort. More of this white stuff was falling through the air. He shook himself, but more of it fell upon him. He sniffed it curiously, then licked some up on his tongue. It bit like fire, and the next instant was gone. This puzzled him. He tried it again, with the same result. The onlookers laughed uproariously and he felt ashamed, he knew not why, for it was his first snow.

Chapter 2

The Law of Club and Fang

BUCK'S FIRST DAY on the Dyea beach was like a nightmare. Every hour was filled with shock and surprise. He had been suddenly jerked from the heart of civilization and flung into the heart of things primordial. No lazy, sun-kissed life was this, with nothing to do but loaf and be bored. Here was neither peace, nor rest, nor a moment's safety. All was confusion and action, and every moment life and limb were in peril. There was imperative need to be constantly alert; for these dogs and men were not town dogs and men. They were savages, all of them, who knew no law but the law of club and fang.

He had never seen dogs fight as these wolfish creatures fought, and his first experience taught him an unforgettable lesson. It is true, it was a vicarious experience, else he would not have lived to profit by it. Curly was the victim. They were camped near the log store, where she, in her friendly way, made advances to a husky dog the size of a full-grown wolf, though not half so large as she. There was no warning, only a leap in like a flash, a metallic clip of teeth, a leap out equally swift, and Curly's face was ripped open from eye to jaw.

It was the wolf manner of fighting, to strike and leap away; but there was more to it than this. Thirty or forty huskies ran to the spot and surrounded the combatants in an intent and silent circle. Buck did not comprehend that silent intentness, nor the eager way with which they were licking their chops. Curly rushed her antagonist, who struck again and leaped aside. He met her next rush with his chest, in a peculiar fashion that tumbled her off her feet. She never regained them. This was what the onlooking huskies had waited for. They closed in upon her, snarling and yelping, and she was buried, screaming with agony, beneath the bristling mass of bodies.

So sudden was it, and so unexpected, that Buck was taken aback. He saw Spitz run out his scarlet tongue in a way he had of laughing; and he saw François, swinging an ax, spring into the mess of dogs. Three men with clubs were helping him to scatter them. It did not take long. Two minutes from the time Curly went down, the last of her assailants were clubbed off. But she lay there limp and lifeless in the bloody, trampled snow, almost literally torn to pieces, the swart half-breed standing over her and cursing horribly. The scene often came back to Buck to trouble him in his sleep. So that was the way. No fair play. Once down, that was the end of you. Well, he would see to it that he never went down. Spitz ran out his tongue and laughed again, and from that moment Buck hated him with a bitter and deathless hatred.

Before he had recovered from the shock caused by the tragic passing of Curly, he received another shock. François fastened upon him an arrangement of straps and buckles. It was a harness, such as he had seen the grooms put on the horses at home. And as he had seen horses work, so he was set to work, hauling François on a sled to the forest that fringed the valley, and returning with a load of firewood. Though his dignity was sorely hurt by thus being made a draft animal, he was too wise to rebel. He buckled down with a will and did his best, though it was all new and strange. François was stern, demanding instant obedience, and by virtue of his whip receiving instant obedience; while Dave, who was an experienced wheeler, nipped Buck's hind quarters whenever he was in error. Spitz was the leader, likewise experienced, and while he could not always get at Buck, he growled sharp reproof now and again, or cunningly threw his weight in the traces to jerk Buck into the way he should go. Buck learned easily, and under the combined tuition of his two mates and François made remarkable progress. Ere they returned to camp he knew enough to stop at "ho," to go ahead at "mush," to swing wide on the bends and to keep clear of the wheeler when the loaded sled shot downhill at their heels.

"T'ree vair' good dogs," François told Perrault. "Dat Buck, heem pool lak hell. I tich heem queek as anyt'ing."

By afternoon, Perrault, who was in a hurry to be on the trail with his dispatches, returned with two more dogs. Billee and Joe he called them, two brothers, and true huskies both. Sons of the one mother though they were, they were as different as day and night. Billee's one fault was his excessive good nature, while Joe was the very opposite, sour and introspective, with a perpetual snarl and a malignant eye. Buck received them in comradely fashion, Dave ignored them, while Spitz proceeded to thrash first one and then the other. Billee wagged his tail appeasingly, turned to run when he saw that appeasement was of no avail, and cried (still appeasingly) when Spitz's sharp teeth scored his flank. But no matter how Spitz circled, Joe whirled around on his heels to face him, mane bristling, ears laid back, lips writhing and snarling, jaws clipping together as fast as he could snap, and eyes diabolically gleaming—the incarnation of belligerent fear. So terrible was his appearance that Spitz was forced to forgo disciplining him; but to cover his own discomfiture he turned upon the inoffensive and wailing Billee and drove him to the confines of the camp.

By evening Perrault secured another dog, an old husky, long and lean and gaunt, with a battle-scarred face and a single eye which flashed a warning of prowess that commanded respect. He was called Sol-leks, which means The Angry One. Like Dave, he asked nothing, gave nothing, expected nothing; and when he marched slowly and deliberately into their midst, even Spitz left him alone. He had one peculiarity which Buck was unlucky enough to discover. He did not like to be approached on his blind side. Of this offense Buck was unwitting guilty, and the first knowledge he had of his indiscretion was when Sol-leks whirled upon him and slashed his shoulder to the bone for three inches up and down. Forever after Buck avoided his blind side, and to the last of their comradeship had no more trouble. His only apparent ambition, like Dave's, was to be left alone; though, as Buck was afterward to learn, each of them possessed one other and even more vital ambition.

That night Buck faced the great problem of sleeping. The tent, illumined by a candle, glowed warmly in the midst of the white plain; and when he, as a matter of course, entered it, both Perrault and

François bombarded him with curses and cooking utensils, till he recovered from his consternation and fled ignominiously into the outer cold. A chill wind was blowing that nipped him sharply and bit with especial venom into his wounded shoulder. He lay down on the snow and attempted to sleep, but the frost soon drove him shivering to his feet. Miserable and disconsolate, he wandered about among the many tents, only to find that one place was as cold as another. Here and there savage dogs rushed upon him, but he bristled his neck hair and snarled (for he was learning fast), and they let him go his way unmolested.

Finally an idea came to him. He would return and see how his own teammates were making out. To his astonishment, they had disappeared. Again he wandered about through the great camp, looking for them, and again he returned. Were they in the tent? No, that could not be, else he would not have been driven out. Then where could they possibly be? With drooping tail and shivering body, very forlorn indeed, he aimlessly circled the tent. Suddenly the snow gave way beneath his forelegs and he sank down. Something wriggled under his feet. He sprang back, bristling and snarling, fearful of the unseen and unknown. But a friendly little yelp reassured him, and he went back to investigate. A whiff of warm air ascended to his nostrils, and there, curled up under the snow in a snug ball, lay Billee. He whined placatingly, squirmed and wriggled to show his good will and intentions, and even ventured, as a bribe for peace, to lick Buck's face with his warm, wet tongue.

Another lesson. So that was the way they did it, eh? Buck confidently selected a spot, and with much fuss and wasted effort proceeded to dig a hole for himself. In a trice the heat from his body filled the confined space and he was asleep. The day had been long and arduous, and he slept soundly and comfortably, though he growled and barked and wrestled with bad dreams.

Nor did he open his eyes till roused by the noises of the waking camp. At first he did not know where he was. It had snowed during the night and he was completely buried. The snow walls pressed him on every side, and a great surge of fear swept through him—the fear of the wild thing for the trap. It was a token that he was harking back through his own life to the lives of his forebears; for he was a civilized dog, an unduly civilized dog, and of his own experience knew no trap and so could not of himself fear it. The muscles of his whole body contracted spasmodically and instinctively the hair on his neck and shoulders stood on end, and with a ferocious snarl he bounded straight up into the blinding day, the snow flying about him in a flashing cloud. Ere he landed on his feet, he saw the white camp spread out before him and knew where he was and remembered all that had passed from the time he went for a stroll with Manuel to the hole he had dug for himself the night before.

A shout from François hailed his appearance. "Wot I say?" the dog driver cried to Perrault. "Dat Buck for sure learn queek as anyt'ing."

Perrault nodded gravely. As courier for the Canadian Government, bearing important dispatches, he was anxious to secure the best dogs, and he was particularly gladdened by the possession of Buck.

Three more huskies were added to the team inside an hour, making a total of nine, and before another quarter of an hour had passed they were in harness and swinging up the trail toward the Dyea Canyon.

Buck was glad to be gone, and though the work was hard he found he did not particularly despise it. He was surprised at the eagerness which animated the whole team and which was communicated to him; but still more surprising was the change wrought in Dave and Sol-leks. They were new dogs, utterly transformed by the harness. All passiveness and unconcern had dropped from them. They were alert and active, anxious that the work should go well, and fiercely irritable with whatever, by delay or confusion, retarded that work. The toil of the traces seemed the supreme expression of their being, and all that they lived for and the only thing in which they took delight.

Dave was wheeler or sled dog, pulling in front of him was Buck, then came Sol-leks; the rest of the team was strung out ahead, single file, to the leader, which position was filled by Spitz.

Buck had been purposely placed between Dave and Sol-leks so that he might receive instruction. Apt scholar that he was, they were equally apt teachers, never allowing him to linger long in error, and enforcing their teaching with their sharp teeth. Dave was fair and very wise. He never nipped Buck without cause, and he never failed to nip him when he stood in need of it. As François's whip backed him up, Buck found it to be cheaper to mend his ways than to retaliate. Once, during a brief halt, when he got tangled in the traces and delayed the start, both Dave and Sol-leks flew at him and administered a sound trouncing. The resulting tangle was even worse, but Buck took good care to keep the traces clear thereafter; and ere the day was done, so well had he mastered his work, his mates about ceased nagging him. François's whip snapped less frequently, and Perrault even honored Buck by lifting up his feet and carefully examining them.

It was a hard day's run, up the Canyon, through Sheep Camp, past the Scales and the timber line, across glaciers and snowdrifts hundreds of feet deep, and over the great Chilkoot Divide, which stands between the salt water and the fresh and guards forbiddingly the sad and lonely North. They made good time down the chain of lakes which fills the craters of extinct volcanoes, and late that night pulled into the huge camp at the head of Lake Bennett, where thousands of gold seekers were building boats against the break-up of the ice in the spring. Buck made his hole in the snow and slept the sleep of the exhausted just, but all too early was routed out in the cold darkness and harnessed with his mates to the sled.

That day they made forty miles, the trail being packed; but the next day, and for many days to follow, they broke their own trail, worked harder, and made poorer time. As a rule, Perrault traveled ahead of the team, packing the snow with webbed shoes to make it easier for them. François, guiding the sled at the gee pole, sometimes exchanged places with him, but not often. Perrault was in a hurry, and he prided himself on his knowledge of ice, which knowledge was indispensable, for the fall ice was very thin, and where there was swift water, there was no ice at all.

Day after day, for days unending, Buck toiled in the traces. Always, they broke camp in the dark, and the first gray of dawn found them hitting the trail with fresh miles reeled off behind them. And always they pitched camp after dark, eating their bit of fish, and crawling to sleep into the snow. Buck was ravenous. The pound and a half of sun-dried salmon which was his ration for each day seemed to go nowhere. He never had enough, and suffered from perpetual hunger pangs. Yet the other dogs, because they weighed less and were born to the life, received a pound only of the fish and managed to keep in good condition.

He swiftly lost the fastidiousness which had characterized his old life. A dainty eater, he found that his mates, finishing first, robbed him of his unfinished ration. There was no defending it. While he was fighting off two or three, it was disappearing down the throats of the others. To remedy this, he ate as fast as they; and, so greatly did hunger compel him, he was not above taking what did not belong to him. He watched and learned. When he saw Pike, one of the new dogs, a clever malingerer and thief, slyly steal a slice of bacon when Perrault's back was turned, he duplicated the performance the following day, getting away with the whole chunk. A great uproar was raised, but he was unsuspected; while Dub, an awkward blunderer who was always getting caught, was punished for Buck's misdeed.

This first theft marked Buck as fit to survive in the hostile Northland environment. It marked his adaptability, his capacity to adjust himself to changing conditions, the lack of which would have meant swift and terrible death. It marked, further, the decay or going to pieces of his moral nature, a vain thing and a handicap in the ruthless struggle for existence. It was all well enough in the Southland, under the law of love and fellowship, to respect private property and personal feelings; but in the Northland, under the law of club and fang, whoso took such things into account was a fool, and in so far as he observed them he would fail to prosper.

Not that Buck reasoned it out. He was fit, that was all, and unconsciously he accommodated himself to the new mode of life. All his days, no matter what the odds, he had never run from a fight. But the club of the man in the red sweater had beaten into him a more fundamental and primitive code. Civilized, he could have died for a moral consideration, say the defense of Judge Miller's riding whip; but the completeness of his de-civilization was now evidenced by his ability to flee from the defense of a moral consideration and so save his hide. He did not steal for joy of it, but because of the clamor of his stomach. He did not rob openly, but stole secretly and cunningly, out of respect for club and fang. In short, the things he did were done because it was easier to do them than not to do them.

His development (or retrogression) was rapid. His muscles became hard as iron, and he grew callous to all ordinary pain. He achieved an internal as well as external economy. He could eat anything, no matter how loathsome or indigestible; and, once eaten, the juices of his stomach extracted the last least particle of nutriment; and his blood carried it to the farthest reaches of his body, building it into the toughest and stoutest of tissues. Sight and scent became remarkably keen while his hearing developed such acuteness that in his sleep he heard the faintest sound and knew whether it heralded peace or peril. He learned to bite the ice out with his teeth when it collected between his toes, and when he was thirsty and there was a thick scum of ice over the water hole, he would break it by rearing and striking it with stiff forelegs. His most conspicuous trait was an ability to scent the wind and forecast it a night in advance. No matter how breathless the air when he dug his nest by tree or bank, the wind that later blew inevitably found him to leeward, sheltered and snug.

And not only did he learn by experience, but

instincts long dead became alive again. The domesticated generations fell from him. In vague ways he remembered back to the youth of the breed, to the time the wild dogs ranged in packs through the primeval forest and killed their meat as they ran it down. It was no task for him to learn to fight with cut and slash and the quick wolf snap. In this manner had fought forgotten ancestors. They quickened the old life within him, and the old tricks which they had stamped into the heredity of the breed were his tricks. They came to him without effort or discovery, as though they had been his always. And when, on the still, cold nights, he pointed his nose at a star and howled long and wolflike, it was his ancestors, dead and dust, pointing nose at star and howling down through the centuries and through him. And his cadences were their cadences, the cadences which voiced their woe and what to them was the meaning of the stillness, and the cold, and dark. Thus, as token of what a puppet thing life is, the ancient song surged through him and he came into his own again; and he came because men had found a yellow metal in the North, and because Manuel was a gardener's helper whose wages did not lap over the needs of his wife and divers small copies of himself.

Chapter 

The Dominant Primordial Beast

THE DOMINANT PRIMORDIAL BEAST was strong in Buck, and under the fierce conditions of trail life it grew and grew. Yet it was a secret growth. His newborn cunning gave him poise and control. He was too busy adjusting himself to the new life to feel at ease, and not only did he not pick fights, but he avoided them whenever possible. A certain deliberateness characterized his attitude. He was not prone to rashness and precipitate action; and in the bitter hatred between him and Spitz he betrayed no impatience, shunned all offensive acts.

On the other hand, possibly because he divined in Buck a dangerous rival, Spitz never lost an opportunity of showing his teeth. He even went out of his way to bully Buck, striving constantly to start the fight which could end only in the death of one or the other. Early in the trip this might have taken place had it not been for an unwonted accident. At the end of this day they made a bleak and miserable camp on the shore of Lake Laberge. Driving snow, a wind that cut like a white-hot knife, and darkness had forced them to grope for a camping place. They could hardly have fared worse. At their backs rose a perpendicular wall of rock, and Perrault and François were compelled to make their fire and spread their sleeping robes on the ice of the lake itself. The tent they had discarded at Dyea in order to travel light. A few sticks of driftwood furnished them with a fire that thawed down through the ice and left them to eat supper in the dark

Close in under the sheltering rock Buck made his nest. So snug and warm was it, that he was loath to leave it when François distributed the fish which he had first thawed over the fire. But when Buck finished his ration and returned, he found his nest occupied. A warning snarl told him that the trespasser was Spitz. Till now Buck had avoided trouble with his enemy, but this was too much. The beast in him roared. He sprang upon Spitz with a fury which surprised them both, and Spitz particularly, for his whole experience with Buck had gone to teach him that his rival was an unusually timid dog, who managed to hold his own only because of his great weight and size.

François was surprised, too, when they shot out in a tangle from the disrupted nest and he divined the cause of the trouble "A-a-ah!" he cried to Buck. "Gif it to heem, by Gar! Gif it to heem, the dirty t'eef!"

Spitz was equally willing. He was crying with sheer rage and eagerness as he circled back and forth for a chance to spring in. Buck was no less eager, and no less cautious, as he likewise circled back and forth for the advantage. But it was then that the unexpected happened, the thing which projected their struggle for supremacy far into the future, past many a weary mile of trail and toil.

An oath from Perrault, the resounding impact of a club upon a bony frame, and a shrill yelp of pain heralded the breaking forth of pandemonium. The camp was suddenly discovered to be alive with skulking furry forms—starving huskies, four or five score of them, who had scented the camp from some Indian village. They had crept in while Buck and Spitz were fighting, and when the two men sprang among them with stout clubs they showed their teeth and fought back. They were crazed by the smell of the food. Perrault found one with head buried in the grub box. His club landed heavily on the gaunt ribs, and the grub box was capsized on the ground. On the instant a score of the famished brutes were scrambling for the bread and bacon. The clubs fell upon them unheeded. They yelped and howled under the rain of blows, but struggled none the less madly till the last crumb had been devoured.

In the meantime the astonished team dogs had burst out of their nests only to be set upon by the fierce invaders. Never had Buck seen such dogs. It seemed as though their bones would burst through their skins. They were mere skeletons, draped loosely in draggled hides, with blazing eyes and slavered fangs. But the hunger madness made them terrifying, irresistible. There was no opposing them. The team dogs were swept back against the cliff at the first onset. Buck was beset by three huskies, and in a trice his head and shoulders were ripped and slashed. The din was frightful. Billee was crying as usual. Dave and Sol-leks, dripping blood from a score of wounds, were fighting bravely side by side. Joe was snapping like a demon. Once, his teeth closed on the foreleg of a husky, and he crunched down through the bone. Pike, the malingerer, leaped upon the crippled animal, breaking its neck with a quick flash of teeth and a jerk. Buck got a frothing adversary by the throat, and was sprayed with blood when his teeth sank through the jugular. The warm taste of it in his mouth goaded him to greater fierceness. He flung himself upon another, and at the same time felt teeth sink into his own throat. It was Spitz, treacherously attacking from the side.

Perrault and François, having cleaned out their part of the camp, hurried to save their sled dogs. The wild wave of famished beasts rolled back before them, and Buck shook himself free. But it was only for a moment. The two men were compelled to run back to save the grub, upon which the huskies returned to the attack on the team. Billee, terrified into bravery, sprang through the savage circle and fled away over the ice. Pike and Dub followed on his heels, with the rest of the team behind. As Buck drew himself together to spring after them, out of the tail of his eye he saw Spitz rush upon him with the evident intention of overthrowing him. Once off his feet and under that mass of huskies, there was no hope for him. But he braced himself to the shock of Spitz's charge, then joined the flight out on the lake.

Later, the nine team dogs gathered together and sought shelter in the forest. Though unpursued, they were in a sorry plight. There was not one who was not wounded in four or five places, while some were wounded grievously. Dub was badly injured in a hind leg; Dolly, the last husky added to the team at Dyea, had a badly torn throat; Joe had lost an eye; while Billee, the good-natured, with an ear chewed and rent to ribbons, cried and whimpered throughout the night. At daybreak they limped warily back to camp, to find the marauders gone and the two men in bad tempers. Fully half their grub supply was gone. The huskies had chewed through the sled lashings and canvas coverings. In fact, nothing, no matter how remotely eatable, had escaped them. They had eaten a pair of Perrault's moose-hide moccasins, chunks out of the leather traces, and even two feet of lash from the end of François's whip. He broke from a mournful contemplation of it to look over his wounded dogs.

"Ah, my frien's," he said softly, "mebbe it mek you mad dog, dose many bites. Mebbe all mad dog, *sacrédam*! Wot you t'ink, eh, Perrault?"

The courier shook his head dubiously. With four hundred miles of trail still between him and Dawson, he could ill afford to have madness break out among his dogs. Two hours of cursing and exertion got the harnesses into shape, and the wound-stiffened team was under way, struggling painfully over the hardest part of the trail they had yet encountered, and for that matter, the hardest between them and Dawson.

The Thirty Mile River was wide open. Its wild water defied the frost, and it was in the eddies only and in the quiet places that the ice held at all. Six days of exhausting toil were required to cover those thirty terrible miles. And terrible they were, for every foot of them was accomplished at the risk of life to dog and man. A dozen times Perrault, nosing the way, broke through the ice bridges, being saved by the long pole he carried, which he so held that it fell each time across the hole made by his body. But a cold snap was on, the thermometer registering fifty below zero, and each time he broke through he was compelled for very life to build a fire and dry his garments.

Nothing daunted him. It was because nothing daunted him that he had been chosen for government courier. He took all manner of risks, resolutely thrusting his little weazened face into the frost and struggling on from dim dawn to dark. He skirted the frowning shores on rim ice that bent and crackled under foot and upon which they dared not halt. Once, the sled broke through, with Dave and Buck, and they were half-frozen and all but drowned by the time they were dragged out. The usual fire was necessary to save them. They were coated solidly with ice, and the two men kept them on the run around the fire, sweating and thawing, so close that they were singed by the flames.

At another time Spitz went through, dragging the whole team after him up to Buck, who strained backward with all his strength, his forepaws on the slippery edge and the ice quivering and snapping all around. But behind him was Dave, likewise straining backward, and behind the sled was François, pulling till his tendons cracked.

Again, the rim ice broke away before and behind, and there was no escape except up the cliff. Perrault scaled it by a miracle, while François prayed for just that miracle; and with every thong and sled lashing and the last bit of harness rove into a long rope, the dogs were hoisted, one by one, to the cliff crest. François came up last, after the sled and load. Then came the search for a place to descend, which descent was ultimately made by the aid of the rope, and night found them back on the river with a quarter of a mile to the day's credit.

By the time they made the Hootalinqua and good ice, Buck was played out. The rest of the dogs were in like condition; but Perrault, to make up lost time, pushed them late and early. The first day they covered thirty-five miles to the Big Salmon, the next day thirty-five more to the Little Salmon; the third day forty miles, which brought them well up toward the Five Fingers.

Buck's feet were not so compact and hard as the feet of the huskies. His had softened during the many generations since the day his last wild ancestor was tamed by a cave dweller or river man. All day long he limped in agony, and camp once made, lay down like a dead dog. Hungry as he was, he would not move to receive his ration of fish, which François had to bring to him. Also, the dog driver rubbed Buck's feet for half an hour each night after supper, and sacrificed the tops of his own moccasins to make four moccasins for Buck. This was a great relief, and Buck caused even the weazened face of Perrault to twist itself into a grin one morning, when François forgot the moccasins and Buck lay on his back, his four feet waving appealingly in the air, and refused to budge without them. Later his feet grew hard to the trail and the worn-out footgear was thrown away.

At the Pelly one morning, as they were harnessing up, Dolly, who had never been conspicuous for anything, went suddenly mad. She announced her condition by a long, heartbreaking wolf howl that sent every dog bristling with fear, then sprang straight for Buck. He had never seen a dog go mad, nor did he have any reason to fear madness; yet he knew that here was horror, and fled away from it in a panic. Straight away he raced, with Dolly, panting and frothing, one leap behind; nor could she gain on him, so great was his terror, nor could he leave her, so great was her madness. He plunged through the wooded breast of the island, flew down to the lower end, crossed a back channel filled with rough ice to another island, gained a third island, curved back to the main river, and in desperation started to cross it. And all the time, though he did not look, he could hear her snarling just one leap behind. François called to him a quarter of a mile away and he doubled back, still one leap ahead, gasping painfully for air and putting all his faith in that François would save him. The dog driver held the ax poised in his hand, and as Buck shot past him the ax crashed down upon mad Dolly's head.

Buck staggered over against the sled, exhausted, sobbing for breath, helpless. This was Spitz's opportunity. He sprang upon Buck, and twice his teeth sank into his unresisting foe and ripped and tore the flesh to the bone. Then François's lash descended, and Buck had the satisfaction of watching Spitz receive the worst whipping as yet administered to any of the teams.

"One devil, dat Spitz," remarked Perrault. "Some dam' day heem keel dat Buck."

"Dat Buck two devils," was François's rejoinder. "All de tam I watch dat Buck I know for sure. Lissen: some dam' fine day heem get mad lak hell an' den heem chew dat Spitz all up an' spit heem out on de snow. Sure. I know."

From then on it was war between them. Spitz, as lead dog and acknowledged master of the team, felt his supremacy threatened by this strange Southland dog. And strange Buck was to him, for of the many Southland dogs he had known, not one had shown up worthily in camp and on trail. They were all too soft, dying under the toil, the frost, and starvation. Buck was the exception. He alone endured and prospered, matching the husky in strength, savagery, and cunning. Then he was a masterful dog and what made him dangerous was the fact that the club of the man in the red sweater had knocked all blind pluck and rashness out of his desire for mastery. He was pre-eminently cunning, and could bide his time with a patience that was nothing less than primitive.

It was inevitable that the clash for leadership

should come. Buck wanted it. He wanted it because it was his nature, because he had been gripped tight by that nameless, incomprehensible pride of the trail and trace—that pride which holds dogs in the toil to the last gasp, which lures them to die joyfully in the harness, and breaks their hearts if they are cut out of the harness. This was the pride of Dave as wheel dog, of Sol-leks as he pulled with all his strength; the pride that laid hold of them at break of camp, transforming them from sour and sullen brutes into straining, eager, ambitious creatures; the pride that spurred them on all day and dropped them at pitch of camp at night, letting them fall back into gloomy unrest and uncontent. This was the pride that bore up Spitz and made him thrash the sled dogs who blundered and shirked in the traces or hid away at harness-up time in the morning. Likewise it was this pride that made him fear Buck as a possible lead dog. And this was Buck's pride, too.

He openly threatened the other's leadership. He came between him and the shirks he should have punished. And he did it deliberately. One night there was a heavy snowfall, and in the morning Pike, the malingerer, did not appear. He was securely hidden in the nest under a foot of snow. François called him and sought him in vain. Spitz was wild with wrath. He raged through the camp, smelling and digging in every likely place, snarling so frightfully that Pike heard and shivered in his hiding place.

But when he was at last unearthed, and Spitz flew at him to punish him, Buck flew, with equal rage, in between. So unexpected was it, and so shrewdly managed, that Spitz was hurled backward and off his feet. Pike, who had been trembling abjectly, took heart at this open mutiny, and sprang upon his overthrown leader. Buck, to whom fair play was a forgotten code, likewise sprang upon Spitz. But François, chuckling at the incident while unswerving in the administration of justice, brought his lash down upon Buck with all his might. This failed to drive Buck from his prostrate rival, and the butt of the whip was brought into play. Half-stunned by the blow, Buck was knocked backward and the lash laid upon him again and again, while Spitz soundly punished the many-times-offending Pike.

In the days that followed, as Dawson grew closer and closer, Buck still continued to interfere between Spitz and the culprits; but he did it craftily, when François was not around. With the covert mutiny of Buck, a general insubordination sprang up and increased. Dave and Sol-leks were unaffected, but the rest of the team went from bad to worse. Things no longer went right. There was continual bickering and jangling. Trouble was always afoot, and at the bottom of it was Buck. He kept François busy, for the dog driver was in constant apprehension of the life-and-death struggle between the two which he knew must take place sooner or later; and on more than one night the sounds of quarreling and strife among the other dogs turned him out of his sleeping robe, fearful that Buck and Spitz were at it.

But the opportunity did not present itself, and they pulled into Dawson one dreary afternoon with the great fight still to come. Here were many men, and countless dogs, and Buck found them all at work. It seemed the ordained order of things that dogs should work. All day they swung up and down the main street in long teams, and in the night their jingling bells still went by. They hauled cabin logs and firewood, freighted up to the mines, and did all manner of work that horses did in the Santa Clara Valley. Here and there Buck met Southland dogs, but in the main they were the wild wolf husky breed. Every night, regularly, at nine, at twelve, at three, they lifted a nocturnal song, a weird and eerie chant, in which it was Buck's delight to join.

With the aurora borealis flaming coldly overhead, or the stars leaping in the frost dance, and the land numb and frozen under its pall of snow, this song of the huskies might have been the defiance of life, only it was pitched in minor key, with long-drawn wailings and half-sobs, and was more the pleading of life, the articulate travail of existence. It was an old song, old as the breed itself—one of the first songs of the younger world in a day when songs were sad. It was invested with the woe of unnumbered generations, this plaint by which Buck was so strangely stirred. When he moaned and sobbed, it was with the pain of living that was of old the pain of his wild fathers, and the fear and mystery of the cold and dark that was to them fear and mystery. And that he should be stirred by it marked the completeness with which he harked back through the ages of fire and roof to the raw beginnings of life in the howling ages.

Seven days from the time they pulled into Dawson, they dropped down the steep bank by the Barracks to the Yukon Trail, and pulled for Dyea and Salt Water. Perrault was carrying dispatches if anything more urgent than those he had brought in; also, the travel pride had gripped him, and he purposed to make the record trip of the year. Several things favored him in this. The week's rest had recuperated the dogs and put them in thorough trim. The trail they had broken into the country was packed hard by later journeyers. And further, the police had arranged in two or three places deposits of grub for dog and man, and he was traveling light.

They made Sixty Mile, which is a fifty-mile run, on the first day; and the second day saw them booming up the Yukon well on their way to Pelly. But such splendid running was achieved not without great trouble and vexation on the part of François. The insidious revolt led by Buck had destroyed the solidarity of the team. It no longer was as one dog leaping in the traces. The encouragement Buck gave the rebels led them into all kinds of petty misdemeanors. No more was Spitz a leader greatly to be feared. The old awe departed, and they grew equal to challenging his authority. Pike robbed him of half a fish one night, and gulped it down under the protection of Buck. Another night Dub and Joe fought Spitz and made him forego the punishment they deserved. And even Billee, the good-natured, was less good-natured, and whined not half so placatingly as in former days. Buck never came near Spitz without snarling and bristling menacingly. In fact, his conduct approached that of a bully, and he was given to swaggering up and down before Spitz's very nose.

The breaking down of discipline likewise affected the dogs in their relations with one another. They quarreled and bickered more than ever among themselves, till at times the camp was a howling bedlam. Dave and Sol-leks alone were unaltered, though they were made irritable by the unending squabbling. François swore strange, barbarous oaths, and stamped the snow in futile rage, and tore his hair. His lash was always singing among the dogs, but it was of small avail. Directly his back was turned they were at it again. He backed up Spitz with his whip, while Buck backed up the remainder of the team. François knew he was behind all the trouble, and Buck knew he knew; but Buck was too clever

ever again to be caught red-handed. He worked faithfully in the harness, for the toil had become a delight to him; yet it was a greater delight slyly to precipitate a fight amongst his mates and tangle the traces.

At the mouth of the Talkeetna, one night after supper, Dub turned up a snowshoe rabbit, blundered it, and missed. In a second the whole team was in full cry. A hundred yards away was a camp of the Northwest Police, with fifty dogs, huskies all, who joined the chase. The rabbit sped down the river, turned off into a small creek, up the frozen bed of which it held steadily. It ran lightly on the surface of the snow, while the dogs ploughed through by main strength. Buck led the pack, sixty strong, around bend after bend, but he could not gain. He lay down low to the race, whining eagerly, his splendid body flashing forward, leap by leap, in the wan, white moonlight. And leap by leap, like some pale frost wraith, the snowshoe rabbit flashed on ahead.

All that stirring of old instincts which at stated periods drives men out from the sounding cities to forest and plain to kill things by chemically propelled leaden pellets, the blood lust, the joy to kill—all this was Buck's, only it was infinitely more intimate. He was ranging at the head of the pack, running the wild thing down, the living meat, to kill with his own teeth and wash his muzzle to the eyes in warm blood.

There is an ecstasy that marks the summit of life, and beyond which life cannot rise. And such is the paradox of living, this ecstasy comes when one is most alive, and it comes as a complete forgetfulness that one is alive. This ecstasy, this forgetfulness of living, comes to the artist, caught up and out of himself in a sheet of flame; it comes to the soldier, war-mad on a stricken field and refusing quarter; and it came to Buck, leading the pack, sounding the old wolf cry, straining after the food that was alive and that fled swiftly before him through the moonlight. He was sounding the deeps of his nature, and of the parts of his nature that were deeper than he, going back into the womb of Time. He was mastered by the sheer surging of life, the tidal wave of being, the perfect joy of each separate muscle, joint, and sinew in that it was everything that was not death, that it was aglow and rampant, expressing itself in movement, flying exultantly under the stars and over the face of dead matter that did not move.

But Spitz, cold and calculating even in his supreme moods, left the pack and cut across a narrow neck of land where the creek made a long bend around. Buck did not know of this, and as he rounded the bend, the frost wraith of a rabbit still flitting before him, he saw another and larger frost wraith leap from the overhanging bank into the immediate path of the rabbit. It was Spitz. The rabbit could not turn, and as the white teeth broke its back in midair it shrieked as loudly as a stricken man may shriek. At sound of this, the cry of Life plunging down from Life's apex in the grip of Death, the full pack at Buck's heels raised a hell's chorus of delight.

Buck did not cry out. He did not check himself, but drove in upon Spitz, shoulder to shoulder, so hard that he missed the throat. They rolled over and over in the Powdery snow. Spitz gained his feet almost as though he had not been overthrown, slashing Buck down the shoulder and leaping clear. Twice his teeth clipped together, like the steel jaws of a trap, as he backed away for better footing, with lean and lifting lips that writhed and snarled.

In a flash Buck knew it. The time had come. It was to the death. As they circled about, snarling, ears laid back, keenly watchful for the advantage, the scene came to Buck with a sense of familiarity. He seemed to remember it all—the white woods, and earth, and moonlight, and the thrill of battle. Over the whiteness and silence brooded a ghostly calm. There was not the faintest whisper of air—nothing moved, not a leaf quivered, the visible breaths of the dogs rising slowly and lingering in the frosty air. They had made short work of the snowshoe rabbit, these dogs that were ill-tamed wolves; and they were now drawn up in an expectant circle. They, too, were silent, their eyes only gleaming and their breaths drifting slowly upward. To Buck it was nothing new or strange, this scene of old time. It was as though it had always been, the wonted way of things.

Spitz was a practiced fighter. From Spitzbergen through the Arctic, and across Canada and the Barrens, he had held his own with all manner of dogs and achieved to mastery over them. Bitter rage was his, but never blind rage. In passion to rend and destroy, he never forgot that his enemy was in like passion to rend and destroy. He never rushed till he was prepared to receive a rush; never attacked till he had first defended that attack.

In vain Buck strove to sink his teeth in the neck of the big white dog. Wherever his fangs struck for the softer flesh, they were countered by the fangs of Spitz. Fang clashed fang, and lips were cut and bleeding, but Buck could not penetrate his enemy's guard. Then he warmed up and enveloped Spitz in a whirlwind of rushes. Time and time again he tried for the snow-white throat, where life bubbled near to the surface, and each time and every time Spitz slashed him and got away. Then Buck took to rushing, as though for the throat, when, suddenly drawing back his head and curving in from the side, he would drive his shoulder at the shoulder of Spitz, as a ram by which to overthrow him. But instead, Buck's shoulder was slashed down each time as Spitz leaped lightly away.

Spitz was untouched, while Buck was streaming with blood and panting hard. The fight was growing desperate. And all the while the silent and wolfish circle waited to finish off whichever dog went down. As Buck grew winded, Spitz took to rushing, and he kept him staggering for footing. Once Buck went over, and the whole circle of sixty dogs started up; but he recovered himself, almost in midair, and the circle sank down again and waited.

But Buck possessed a quality that made for greatness—imagination. He fought by instinct, but he could fight by head as well. He rushed, as though attempting the old shoulder trick, but at the last instant swept low to the snow and in. His teeth closed on Spitz's left foreleg. There was a crunch of breaking bone, and the white dog faced him on three legs. Thrice he tried to knock him over, then repeated the trick and broke the right foreleg. Despite the pain and helplessness, Spitz struggled madly to keep up. He saw the silent circle, with gleaming eyes, lolling tongues, and silvery breaths drifting upward, closing in upon him as he had seen similar circles close in upon beaten antagonists in the past. Only this time he was the one who was beaten.

There was no hope for him. Buck was inexorable. Mercy was a thing reserved for gentler climes. He maneuvered for the final rush. The circle had tightened till he could feel the breaths of the huskies on his flanks. He could see them, beyond Spitz and to either side, half-crouching for the spring, their eyes fixed upon him. A pause seemed to fall. Every animal was motionless as though turned to stone.

Only Spitz quivered and bristled as he staggered back and forth, snarling with horrible menace, as though to frighten off impending death. Then Buck sprang in and out; but while he was in, shoulder had at last squarely met shoulder. The dark circle became a dot on the moonflooded snow as Spitz disappeared from view. Buck stood and looked on, the successful champion, the dominant primordial beast who had made his kill and found it good.

Chapter 4

Who Has Won to Mastership

"EH? WOT I SAY? I spik true w'en I say dat Buck two devils."

This was François's speech next morning when he discovered Spitz missing and Buck covered with wounds. He drew him to the fire and by its light pointed them out.

"Dat Spitz fight lak hell," said Perrault, as he surveyed the gaping rips and cuts.

"An' dat Buck fight lak two hells," was François's answer. "An' now we make good time. No more Spitz, no more trouble, sure."

While Perrault packed the camp outfit and loaded the sled, the dog driver proceeded to harness the dogs. Buck trotted up to the place Spitz would have occupied as leader; but François, not noticing him, brought Sol-leks to the coveted position. In his judgment, Sol-leks was the best lead dog left. Buck sprang upon Sol-leks in a fury, driving him back and standing in his place.

"Eh? eh?" François cried, slapping his thighs gleefully. "Look at dat Buck. Heem keel dat Spitz, heem t'ink to take the job."

"Go 'way, Chook!" he cried, but Buck refused to budge.

He took Buck by the scruff of the neck, and though the dog growled threateningly, dragged him to one side and replaced Sol-leks. The old dog did not like it, and showed plainly that he was afraid of Buck. François was obdurate, but when he turned his back Buck again displaced Sol-leks, who was not at all unwilling to go.

François was angry. "Now, by Gar, I feex you!" he cried, coming back with a heavy club in his hand.

Buck remembered the man in the red sweater, and retreated slowly; nor did he attempt to charge in when Sol-leks was once more brought forward. But he circled just beyond the range of the club, snarling with bitterness and rage; and while he circled he watched the club so as to dodge it if thrown by François, for he was become wise in the way of clubs.

The driver went about his work, and he called to Buck when he was ready to put him in his old place in front of Dave. Buck retreated two or three steps. François followed him up, whereupon he again retreated. After some time of this, François threw down the club, thinking that Buck feared a thrashing. But Buck was in open revolt. He wanted, not to escape a clubbing, but to have the leadership. It was his by right. He had earned it, and he would not be content with less.

Perrault took a hand. Between them they ran him about for the better part of an hour. They threw clubs at him. He dodged. They cursed him, and his fathers and mothers before him, and all his seed to come after him down to the remotest generation, and every hair on his body and drop of blood in his veins;

and he answered curse with snarl and kept out of their reach. He did not try to run away, but retreated around and around the camp, advertising plainly that when his desire was met, he would come in and be good.

François sat down and scratched his head. Perrault looked at his watch and swore. Time was flying, and they should have been on the trail an hour gone. François scratched his head again. He shook it and grinned sheepishly at the courier, who shrugged his shoulders in sign that they were beaten. Then François went up to where Sol-leks stood and called to Buck. Buck laughed, as dogs laugh, yet kept his distance. François unfastened Sol-leks's traces and put him back in his old place. The team stood harnessed to the sled in an unbroken line, ready for the trail. There was no place for Buck save at the front. Once more François called, and once more Buck laughed and kept away.

"T'row down de club," Perrault commanded.

François complied, whereupon Buck trotted in, laughing triumphantly, and swung around into position at the head of the team. His traces were fastened, the sled broken out, and with both men running they dashed out on to the river trail.

Highly as the dog driver had forevalued Buck, with his two devils, he found, while the day was yet young, that he had undervalued. At a bound Buck took up the duties of leadership; and where judgment was required, and quick thinking and quick acting, he showed himself the superior even of Spitz, of whom François had never seen an equal.

But it was in giving the law and making his mates live up to it that Buck excelled. Dave and Sol-leks did not mind the change in leadership. It was none of their business. Their business was to toil, and toil mightily, in the traces. So long as that were not interfered with, they did not care what happened. Billee, the good natured, could lead for all they cared, so long as he kept order. The rest of the team, however, had grown unruly during the last days of Spitz, and their surprise was great now that Buck proceeded to lick them into shape.

Pike, who pulled at Buck's heels, and who never put an ounce more of his weight against the breastband than he was compelled to do, was swiftly and repeatedly shaken for loafing; and ere the first day was done he was pulling more than ever before in his life. The first night in camp, Joe, the sour one, was punished roundly—a thing that Spitz had never succeeded in doing. Buck simply smothered him by virtue of superior weight, and cut him up till he ceased snapping and began to whine for mercy.

The general tone of the team picked up immediately. It recovered its old-time solidarity, and once more the dogs leaped as one dog in the traces. At the Rink Rapids two native huskies, Teek and Koona, were added; and the celerity with which Buck broke them in took away Fançois's breath.

"Nevaire such a dog as dat Buck!" he cried. "No, nevaire! Heem worth one t'ousan' dollair, by Gar! Eh? Wot you say, Perrault?"

And Perrault nodded. He was ahead of the record then, and gaining day by day. The trail was in excellent condition, well packed and hard, and there was no new-fallen snow with which to contend. It was not too cold. The temperature dropped to fifty below zero and remained there the whole trip. The men rode and ran by turn, and the dogs were kept on the jump, with but infrequent stoppages.

The Thirty Mile River was comparatively coated with ice, and they covered in one day going out what had taken them ten days coming in. In one run they made a sixty-mile dash from the foot of Lake Laberge to the Whitehorse Rapids. Across Marsh, Tagish, and Bennett (seventy miles of lakes), they flew so fast that the man whose turn it was to run towed behind the sled at the end of a rope. And on the last night of the second week they topped White Pass and dropped down the sea slope with the lights of Skagway and of the shipping at their feet.

It was a record run. Each day for fourteen days they had averaged forty miles. For three days Perrault and François threw chests up and down the main street of Skagway and were deluged with invitations to drink, while the team was the constant center of a worshipful crowd of dog busters and mushers. Then three or four Western bad men aspired to clean out the town, were riddled like pepperboxes for their pains, and public interest turned to other idols. Next came official orders. François called Buck to him, threw his arms around him, wept over him. And that was the last of François and Perrault. Like other men, they passed out of Buck's life for good.

A Scotch half-breed took charge of him and his mates, and in company with a dozen other dog teams he started back over the weary trail to Dawson. It was no light running now, nor record time, but heavy toil each day, with a heavy load behind; for this was the mail train, carrying word from the world to the men who sought gold under the shadow of the Pole.

Buck did not like it, but he bore up well to the work, taking pride in it after the manner of Dave and Sol-leks, and seeing that his mates, whether they prided in it or not, did their fair share. It was a monotonous life, operating with machinelike regularity. One day was very like another. At a certain time each morning the cooks turned out, fires were built, and breakfast was eaten. Then, while some broke camp, others harnessed the dogs, and they were under way an hour or so before the darkness fell which gave warning of dawn. At night, camp was made. Some pitched the flies, others cut firewood and pine boughs for the beds, and still others carried water or ice for the cooks. Also, the dogs were fed. To them, this was the one feature of the day, though it was good to loaf around, after the fish was eaten, for an hour or so with the other dogs, of which there were five score and odd. There were fierce fighters among them, but three battles with the fiercest brought Buck to mastery, so that when he bristled and showed his teeth they got out of his way.

Best of all, perhaps, he loved to lie near the fire, hind legs crouched under him, forelegs stretched out in front, head raised, and eyes blinking dreamily at the flames. Sometimes he thought of Judge Miller's big house in the sun-kissed Santa Clara Valley, and of the cement swimming tank, and Ysabel, the Mexican hairless, and Toots, the Japanese pug; but oftener he remembered the man in the red sweater, the death of Curly, the great fight with Spitz, and the good things he had eaten or would like to eat. He was not homesick. The Sunland was very dim and distant, and such memories had no power over him. Far more potent were the memories of his heredity that gave things he had never seen before a seeming familiarity; the instincts (which were but the memories of his ancestors become habits) which had lapsed in later days, and still later, in him, quickened and became alive again.

Sometimes as he crouched there, blinking dreamily at the flames, it seemed that the flames were of another fire, and that as he crouched by this other fire he saw another and different man from the half-breed cook before him. This other man was shorter of leg and longer of arm, with muscles that were stringy and knotty rather than rounded and swelling. The hair of this man was long and matted, and his head slanted back under it from the eyes. He uttered strange sounds, and seemed very much afraid of the darkness, into which he peered continually, clutching in his hand, which hung midway between knee and foot, a stick with a heavy stone made fast to the end. He was all but naked, a ragged and firescorched skin hanging partway down his back, but on his body there was much hair. In some places, across the chest and shoulders and down the outside of the arms and thighs, it was matted into almost a thick fur. He did not stand erect, but with trunk inclined forward from the hips, on legs that bent at the knees. About his body there was a peculiar springiness, or resiliency, almost catlike, and a quick alertness as of one who lived in perpetual fear of things seen and unseen.

At other times this hairy man squatted by the fire with head between his legs and slept. On such occasions his elbows were on his knees, his hands clasped above his head as though to shed rain by the hairy arms. And beyond that fire, in the circling darkness Buck could see many gleaming coals, two by two, always two by two, which he knew to be the eyes of great beasts of prey. And he could hear the crashing of their bodies through the undergrowth, and the noises they made in the night. And dreaming there by the Yukon bank, with lazy eyes blinking at the fire, these sounds and sights of another world would make the hair to rise along his back and stand on end across his shoulders and up his neck, till he whimpered low and suppressedly, or growled softly, and the half-breed cook shouted at him, "Hey, you

Buck, wake up!" Whereupon the other world would vanish and the real world come into his eyes, and he would get up and yawn and stretch as though he had been asleep.

It was a hard trip, with the mail behind them, and the heavy work wore them down. They were short of weight and in poor condition when they made Dawson, and should have had a ten days' or a week's rest at least. But in two days' time they dropped down the Yukon bank from the Barracks, loaded with letters for the outside. The dogs were tired, the drivers grumbling, and to make matters worse, it snowed every day. This meant a soft trail, greater friction on the runners, and heavier pulling for the dogs; yet the drivers were fair through it all, and did their best for the animals.

Each night the dogs were attended to first. They ate before the drivers ate, and no man sought his sleeping robe till he had seen to the feet of the dogs he drove. Still, their strength went down. Since the beginning of the winter they had traveled eighteen hundred miles, dragging sleds the whole weary distance; and eighteen hundred miles will tell upon life of the toughest. Buck stood it, keeping his mates up to their work and maintaining discipline, though he, too, was very tired. Billee cried and whimpered regularly in his sleep each night. Joe was sourer than ever, and Sol-leks was unapproachable, blind side or other side.

But it was Dave who suffered most of all. Something had gone wrong with him. He became more morose and irritable, and when camp was pitched at once made his nest, where his driver fed him. Once out of the harness and down, he did not get on his feet again till harness-up time in the morning. Sometimes, in the traces, when jerked by a sudden stoppage of the sled, or by straining to start it, he would cry out with pain. The driver examined him, but could find nothing. All the drivers became interested in his case. They talked it over at mealtime, and over their last pipes before going to bed, and one night they held a consultation. He was brought from his nest to the fire and was pressed and prodded till he cried out many times. Something was wrong inside, but they could locate no broken bones, could not make it out.

By the time Cassiar Bar was reached, he was so weak that he was falling repeatedly in the traces. The Scotch half-breed called a halt and took him out of the team, making the next dog, Sol-leks, fast to the sled. His intention was to rest Dave, letting him run free behind the sled. Sick as he was, Dave resented being taken out, grunting and growling while the traces were unfastened, and whimpering brokenheartedly when he saw Sol-leks in the position he had held and served so long. For the pride of trace and trail was his, and, sick unto death, he could not bear that another dog should do his work.

When the sled started, he floundered in the soft snow alongside the beaten trail, attacking Sol-leks with his teeth, rushing against him and trying to thrust him off into the soft snow on the other side, striving to leap inside his traces and get between him and the sled, and all the while whining and yelping and crying with grief and pain. The half-breed tried to drive him away with the whip; but he paid no heed to the stinging lash and the man had not the heart to strike harder. Dave refused to run quietly on the trail behind the sled, where the going was easy, but continued to flounder alongside in the soft snow, where the going was most difficult, till exhausted. Then he fell, and lay where he fell, howling lugubriously as the long train of sleds churned by.

With the last remnant of his strength he managed to stagger along behind till the train made another stop, when he floundered past the sleds to his own, where he stood alongside Sol-leks. His driver lingered a moment to get a light for his pipe from the man behind. Then he returned and started his dogs. They swung out on the trail with remarkable lack of exertion, turned their heads uneasily, and stopped in surprise. The driver was surprised, too; the sled had not moved. He called his comrades to witness the sight. Dave had bitten through both of Sol-leks's traces, and was standing directly in front of the sled in his proper place.

He pleaded with his eyes to remain there. The driver was perplexed. His comrades talked of how a dog could break its heart through being denied the work that killed it, and recalled instances they had known, where dogs, too old for the toil, or injured, had died because they were cut out of the traces. Also, they held it a mercy, since Dave was to die anyway, that he should die in the traces, heart easy and content. So he was harnessed in again, and proudly he pulled as of old, though more than once he cried out involuntarily from the bite of his inward hurt. Several times he fell down and was dragged in the traces, and once the sled ran upon him so that he limped thereafter in one of his hind legs.

But he held out till camp was reached, when his driver made a place for him by the fire. Morning found him too weak to travel. At harness-up time he tried to crawl to his driver. By convulsive efforts he got on his feet, staggered, and fell. Then he wormed his way forward slowly toward where the harnesses were being put on his mates. He would advance his forelegs and drag up his body with a sort of hitching movement, when he would advance his forelegs and hitch ahead again for a few more inches. His strength left him, and the last his mates saw of him he lay gasping in the snow and yearning toward them. But they could hear him mournfully howling till they passed out of sight behind a belt of river timber.

Here the train was halted. The Scotch half-breed slowly retraced his steps to the camp they had left. The men ceased talking. A revolver shot rang out. The man came back hurriedly. The whips snapped, the bells tinkled merrily, the sleds churned along the trail; but Buck knew, and every dog knew, what had taken place behind the belt of river trees.

Chapter 5

The Toil of Trace and Trail

THIRTY DAYS from the time it left Dawson, the Salt Water Mail, with Buck and his mates at the fore, arrived at Skagway. They were in a wretched state, worn out and worn down. Buck's one hundred and forty pounds had dwindled to one hundred and fifteen. The rest of his mates, though lighter dogs, had relatively lost more weight than he. Pike, the malingerer, who, in his lifetime of deceit, had often successfully feigned a hurt leg, was now limping in earnest. Sol-leks was limping, and Dub was suffering from a wrenched shoulder blade.

They were all terribly footsore. No spring or rebound was left in them. Their feet fell heavily on the trail, jarring their bodies and doubling the fatigue of a day's travel. There was nothing the matter with them except that they were dead tired. It was not the dead-tiredness that comes through brief and excessive effort, from which recovery is a matter of hours; but it was the dead-tiredness that comes through the slow and prolonged strength drainage of months of toil. There was no power of recuperation left, no reserve strength to call upon. It had been all used, the last least bit of it. Every muscle, every fiber, every cell, was tired, dead tired. And there was reason for it. In less than five months they had traveled twenty-five hundred miles, during the last eighteen hundred of which they had had but five days' rest. When they arrived at Skagway they were apparently on their last legs. They could barely keep the traces taut, and on the downgrades just managed to keep out of the way of the sled.

"Mush on, poor sore feets," the driver encouraged them as they tottered down the main street of Skagway. "Dis is de las'. Den we get one long res' Eh? For sure. One bully long res'."

The drivers confidently expected a long stop-over. Themselves, they had covered twelve hundred miles with two days' rest, and in the nature of reason and common justice they deserved an interval of loafing. But so many were the men who had rushed into the Klondike, and so many were the sweethearts, wives, and kin that had not rushed in, that the congested mail was taking on Alpine proportions; also, there were official orders. Fresh batches of Hudson Bay dogs were to take the places of those worthless for the trail. The worthless ones were to be got rid of, and, since dogs count for little against dollars, they were to be sold.

Three days passed, by which time Buck and his mates found how really tired and weak they were. Then, on the morning of the fourth day, two men from the States came along and bought them, harness and all, for a song. The men addressed each other as Hal and Charles. Charles was a middle-aged, lightish-colored man, with weak and watery eyes and a mustache that twisted fiercely and vigorously up, giving the lie to the limply drooping lip it concealed. Hal was a youngster of nineteen or twenty, with a big Colt's revolver and a hunting knife strapped about him on a belt that fairly bristled with cartridges. This belt was the most salient thing about him. It advertised his callowness—a callowness sheer and unutterable. Both men were manifestly out of place, and why such as they should adventure the North is part of the mystery of things that passes understanding.

Buck heard the chaffering, saw the money pass between the man and the Government agent, and knew that the Scotch half-breed and the mail-train drivers were passing out of his life on the heels of Perrault and François and the others who had gone before. When driven with his mates to the new owners' camp, Buck saw a slipshod and slovenly affair, tent half-stretched, dishes unwashed, everything in disorder; also, he saw a woman. Mercedes the men called her. She was Charles's wife and Hal's sister—a nice family party.

Buck watched them apprehensively as they proceeded to take down the tent and load the sled. There was a great deal of effort about their manner, but no businesslike method. The tent was rolled into an awkward bundle three times as large as it should have been. The tin dishes were packed away unwashed. Mercedes continually fluttered in the way of her men and kept up an unbroken chattering of remonstrance and advice. When they put a clothes sack on the front of the sled, she suggested it should go on the back; and when they had put it on the back, and covered it over with a couple of other bundles, she discovered overlooked articles which could abide nowhere else but in that very sack, and they unloaded again.

Three men from a neighboring tent came out and

looked on, grinning and winking at one another.

"You've got a right smart load as it is," said one of them; "and it's not me should tell you your business, but I wouldn't tote that tent along if I was you."

"Undreamed of!" cried Mercedes, throwing up her hands in dainty dismay. "However in the world could I manage without a tent?"

"It's springtime, and you won't get any more cold weather," the man replied.

She shook her head decidedly, and Charles and Hal put the last odds and ends an top the mountainous load.

"Think it'll ride?" one of the men asked.

"Why shouldn't it?" Charles demanded rather shortly.

"Oh, that's all right, that's all right," the man hastened meekly to say. "I was just a-wonderin', that is all. It seemed a mite top heavy."

Charles turned his back and drew the lashings down as well as he could, which was not in the least well.

"An' of course the dogs can hike along all day with that contraption behind them," affirmed a second of the men.

"Certainly," said Hal, with freezing politeness, taking hold of the gee pole with one hand and swinging his whip from the other. "Mush!" he shouted. "Mush on there!"

The dogs sprang against the breastbands, strained hard for a few moments, then relaxed. They were unable to move the sled.

"The lazy brutes, I'll show them," he cried, preparing to lash out at them with the whip.

But Mercedes interfered, crying, "Oh, Hal, you mustn't," as she caught hold of the whip and wrenched it from him. "The poor dears! Now you must promise you won't be harsh with them for the rest of the trip, or I won't go a step."

"Precious lot you know about dogs," her brother sneered; "and I wish you'd leave me alone. They're lazy, I tell you, and you've got to whip them to get anything out of them. That's their way. You ask anyone. Ask one of those men."

Mercedes looked at them imploringly, untold repugnance at sight of pain written in her pretty face.

"They're weak as water, if you want to know," came the reply from one of the men. "Plumb tuckered out, that's what's the matter. They need a rest."

"Rest be blanked," said Hal, with his beardless lips; and Mercedes said, "Oh!" in pain and sorrow at the oath.

But she was a clannish creature, and rushed at once to the defense of her brother. "Never mind that man," she said pointedly. "You're driving our dogs, and you do what you think best with them."

Again Hal's whip fell upon the dogs. They threw themselves against the breastbands, dug their feet into the packed snow, got down low to it, and put forth all their strength. The sled held as though it were an anchor. After two efforts, they stood still, panting. The whip was whistling savagely, when once more Mercedes interfered. She dropped on her knees before Buck, with tears in her eyes, and put her arms around his neck.

"You poor, poor dears," she cried sympathetically, "why don't you pull hard?—then you wouldn't be whipped." Buck did not like her, but he was feeling too miserable to resist her, taking it as part of the day's miserable work.

One of the onlookers, who had been clenching his

teeth to suppress hot speech, now spoke up:

"It's not that I care a whoop what becomes of you, but for the dogs' sakes I just want to tell you, you can help them a mighty lot by breaking out that sled. The runners are froze fast. Throw your weight against the gee pole, right and left, and break it out."

A third time the attempt was made, but this time, following the advice, Hal broke out the runners which had been frozen to the snow. The overloaded and unwieldy sled forged ahead, Buck and his mates struggling frantically under the rain of blows. A hundred yards ahead the path turned and sloped steeply into the main street. It would have required an experienced man to keep the top-heavy sled upright, and Hal was not such a man. As they swung on the turn the sled went over, spilling half its load through the loose lashings. The dogs never stopped. The lightened sled bounded on its side behind them. They were angry because of the ill treatment they had received and the unjust load. Buck was raging. He broke into a run, the team following his lead. Hal cried "Whoa! whoa!" but they gave no heed. He tripped and was pulled off his feet. The capsized sled ground over him, and the dogs dashed up the street, adding to the gaiety of Skagway as they scattered the remainder of the outfit along its chief thoroughfare.

Kindhearted citizens caught the dogs and gathered up the scattered belongings. Also, they gave advice. Half the load and twice the dogs, if they ever expected to reach Dawson, was what was said. Hal and his sister and brother-in-law listened unwillingly, pitched tent, and overhauled the outfit. Canned goods were turned out that made men laugh, for canned goods on the Long Trail are a thing to dream about. "Blankets for a hotel," quoth one of the men who laughed and helped. "Half as many is too much;

get rid of them. Throw away that tent, and all those dishes—who's going to wash them anyway? Good Lord, do you think you're traveling on a Pullman?"

And so it went, the inexorable elimination of the superfluous. Mercedes cried when her clothes bags were dumped on the ground and article after article was thrown out. She cried in general, and she cried in particular over each discarded thing. She clasped hands about knees, rocking back and forth broken-heartedly. She averred she would not go an inch, not for a dozen Charleses. She appealed to everybody and to everything, finally wiping her eyes and proceeding to cast out even articles of apparel that were imperative necessaries. And in her zeal, when she had finished with her own, she attacked the belongings of her men and went through them like a tornado.

This accomplished, the outfit, though cut in half, was still a formidable bulk. Charles and Hal went out in the evening and bought six Outside dogs. These, added to the six of the original team, and Teek and Koona, the huskies obtained at the Rink Rapids on the record trip, brought the team up to fourteen. But the Outside dogs, though practically broken in since their landing, did not amount to much. Three were short-haired pointers, one was a Newfoundland, and the other two were mongrels of indeterminate breed. They did not seem to know anything, these newcomers. Buck and his comrades looked upon them with disgust, and though he speedily taught them their places and what not to do, he could not teach them what to do. They did not take kindly to trace and trail. With the exception of the two mongrels, they were bewildered and spirit-broken by the strange, savage environment in which they found themselves and by the ill treatment they had received. The two mongrels were without spirit at all; bones were the only things breakable about them.

With the newcomers hopeless and forlorn, and the old team worn out by twenty-five hundred miles of continuous trail, the outlook was anything but bright. The two men, however, were quite cheerful. And they were proud, too. They were doing the thing in style, with fourteen dogs. They had seen other sleds depart over the Pass for Dawson, or come in from Dawson, but never had they seen a sled with so many as fourteen dogs. In the nature of Arctic travel there was a reason why fourteen dogs should not drag one sled, and that was that one sled could not carry the food for fourteen dogs. But Charles and Hal did not know this. They had worked the trip out with a pencil, so much to a dog, so many dogs, so many days, Q.E.D. Mercedes looked over their shoulders and nodded comprehensively, it was all so very simple.

Late next morning Buck led the long team up the street. There was nothing lively about it, no snap or go in him and his fellows. They were starting dead weary. Four times he had covered the distance between Salt Water and Dawson, and the knowledge that, jaded and tired, he was facing the same trail once more, made him bitter. His heart was not in the work, nor was the heart of any dog. The Outsides were timid and frightened, the Insides without confidence in their masters.

Buck felt vaguely that there was no depending upon these two men and the woman. They did not know how to do anything, and as the days went by it became apparent that they could not learn. They were slack in all things, without order or discipline. It took them half the night to pitch a slovenly camp, and half the morning to break that camp and get the sled loaded in fashion so slovenly that for the rest of the day they were occupied in stopping and rearranging the load. Some days they did not make ten miles. On other days they were unable to get started at all. And on no day did they succeed in making more than half the distance used by the men as a basis in their dog-food computation.

It was inevitable that they should go short on dog food. But they hastened it by overfeeding, bringing the day nearer when underfeeding would commence. The Outside dogs, whose digestions had not been trained by chronic famine to make the most of little, had voracious appetites. And when, in addition to this, the worn-out huskies pulled weakly, Hal decided that the orthodox ration was too small. He doubled it. And to cap it all, when Mercedes, with tears in her pretty eyes and a quaver in her throat, could not cajole him into giving the dogs still more, she stole from the fish sacks and fed them slyly. But it was not food that Buck and the huskies needed, but rest. And though they were making poor time, the heavy load they dragged sapped their strength severely.

Then came the underfeeding. Hal awoke one day to the fact that his dog food was half gone and the distance only quarter covered; further, that for love or money no additional dog food was to be obtained. So he cut down even the orthodox ration and tried to increase the day's travel. His sister and brother-in-law seconded him; but they were frustrated by their heavy outfit and their own incompetence. It was a simple matter to give the dogs less food; but it was impossible to make the dogs travel faster, while their own ability to get under way earlier in the morning prevented them from traveling longer hours. Not only did they not know how to work dogs, but they did not know how to work themselves.

The first to go was Dub. Poor blundering thief that he was, always getting caught and punished, he had none the less been a faithful worker. His wrenched shoulder blade, untreated and unrested, went from bad to worse, till finally Hal shot him with the big Colt's revolver. It is a saying of the country that an outside dog starves to death on the ration of the husky, so the six Outside dogs under Buck could do no less than die on half the ration of the husky. The Newfoundland went first, followed by the three short-haired pointers, the two mongrels hanging more grittily on to life, but going in the end.

By this time all the amenities and gentlenesses of the Southland had fallen away from the three people. Shorn of its glamour and romance, Arctic travel became to them a reality too harsh for their manhood and womanhood. Mercedes ceased weeping over the dogs, being too occupied with weeping over herself and with quarreling with her husband and brother. To quarrel was the one thing they were never too weary to do. Their irritability arose out of their misery, increased with it, doubled upon it, outdistanced it. The wonderful patience of the trail which comes to men who toil hard and suffer sore, and remain sweet of speech and kindly, did not come to these two men and the woman. They had no inkling of such a patience. They were stiff and in pain; their muscles ached, their bones ached, their very hearts ached; and because of this they became sharp of speeeh, and hard words were first on their lips in the morning and last at night.

Charles and Hal wrangled whenever Mercedes gave them a chance. It was the cherished belief of each that he did more than his share of the work, and neither forbore to speak this belief at every opportunity. Sometimes Mercedes sided with her husband, sometimes with her brother. The result was a beautiful and unending family quarrel. Starting from a dispute as to which should chop a few sticks for the fire (a dispute which concerned only Charles and Hal), presently would be lugged in the rest of the family, fathers, mothers, uncles, cousins, people thousands of miles away, and some of them dead. That Hal's views on art, or the sort of society plays his mother's brother wrote, should have anything to do with the chopping of a few sticks af firewood, passes comprehension; nevertheless the quarrel was as likely to tend in that direction as in the direction of Charles's political prejudices. And that Charles's sister's tale-bearing tongue should be relevant to the building of a Yukon fire was apparent only to Mercedes, who disburdened herself of copious opinions upon that topic, and incidentally upon a few other traits unpleasantly peculiar to her husband's family. In the meantime the fire remained unbuilt, the camp half pitched, and the dogs unfed.

Mercedes nursed a special grievance—the grievance of sex; She was pretty and soft, and had been chivalrously treated all her days. But the present treatment by her husband and brother was everything save chivalrous. It was her custom to be helpless. They complained. Upon which impeachment of what to her was her most essential sex-prerogative, she made their lives unendurable. She no longer considered the dogs, and because she was sore and tired, she persisted in riding on the sled. She was pretty and soft, but she weighed one hundred and twenty pounds—a lusty last straw to the load dragged by the weak and starving animals. She rode for days, till they fell in the traces and the sled stood still. Charles and Hal begged her to get off and walk, pleaded with her, entreated, the while she wept and importuned Heaven with a recital of their brutality.

On one occasion they took her off the sled by main strength. They never did it again. She let her legs go limp like a spoiled child, and sat down on the trail. They went on their way, but she did not move. After they had traveled three miles they unloaded the sled, came back for her, and by main strength put her on the sled again.

In the excess of their own misery they were callous to the suffering of their animals. Hal's theory, which he practiced on others, was that one must get hardened. He had started out preaching it to his sister and brother-in-law. Failing there, he hammered it into the dogs with a club. At the Five Fingers the dog food gave out, and a toothless old squaw offered to trade them a few pounds of frozen horse hide for the Colt's revolver that kept the big hunting knife company at Hal's hip. A poor substitute for food was this hide, just as it had been stripped from the starved horses of the cattlemen six months back. In its frozen state it was more like strips of galvanized iron, and when a dog wrestled it into his stomach it thawed into thin and innutritious leathery strings and into a mass of short hair, irritating and indigestible.

And through it all Buck staggered along at the head of the team as in a nightmare. He pulled when he could; when he could no longer pull, he fell down and remained down till blows from whip or club drove him to his feet again. All the stiffness and gloss had gone out of his beautiful furry coat. The hair hung down, limp and draggled, or matted with dried blood where Hal's club had bruised him. His muscles had wasted away to knotty strings, and the flesh pads had disappeared, so that each rib and every bone in his frame were outlined cleanly through the loose hide that was wrinkled in folds of emptiness. It was heartbreaking, only Buck's heart was unbreakable. The man in the red sweater had proved that.

As it was with Buck, so was it with his mates. They were perambulating skeletons. There were seven altogether, including him. In their very great misery they had become insensible to the bite of the lash or the bruise of the club. The pain of the beating was dull and distant, just as the things their eyes saw and their ears heard seemed dull and distant. They were not half living, or quarter living. They were simply so many bags of bones in which sparks of life fluttered faintly. When a halt was made, they dropped down in the traces like dead dogs, and the spark dimmed and paled and seemed to go out. And when the club or whip fell upon them, the spark fluttered feebly up, and they tottered to their feet and staggered on.

There came a day when Billee the good-natured, fell and could not rise. Hal had traded off his revolver, so he took the ax and knocked Billee on the head as he lay in the traces, then cut the carcass out of the harness and dragged it to one side. Buck saw, and his mates saw, and they knew that this thing was very close to them. On the next day Koona went, and but five of them remained: Joe, too far gone to be malignant; Pike, crippled and limping, only half conscious and not conscious enough longer to malinger; Sol-leks, the one-eyed, still faithful to the toil of trace and trail, and mournful in that he had so little strength with which to pull; Teek, who had not traveled so far that winter and who was now beaten more than the others because he was fresher; and Buck, still at the head of the team, but no longer enforcing discipline or striving to enforce it, blind with weakness half the time and keeping the trail by the loom of it and by the dim feel of his feet.

It was beautiful spring weather, but neither dogs nor humans were aware of it. Each day the sun rose earlier and set later. It was dawn by three in the morning, and twilight lingered till nine at night. The whole long day was a blaze of sunshine. The ghostly winter silence had given way to the great spring murmur of awakening life. This murmur arose from all the land, fraught with the joy of living. It came from the things that lived and moved again, things which had been as dead and which had not moved during the long months of frost. The sap was rising in the pines. The willows and aspens were bursting out in young buds. Shrubs and vines were putting on fresh garbs of green. Crickets sang in the nights, and in the days all manner of creeping, crawling things rustled forth into the sun. Partridges and woodpeckers were booming and knocking in the forest. Squirrels were chattering, birds singing, and overhead honked the wild fowl driving up from the south in cunning wedges that split the air.

From every hill slope came the trickle of running water, the music of unseen fountains. All things were thawing, bending, snapping. The Yukon was straining to break loose the ice that bound it down. It ate away from beneath; the sun ate from above. Air holes formed, fissures sprang and spread apart, while thin sections of ice fell through bodily into the river. And amid all this bursting, rending, throbbing of awakening life, under the blazing sun and through the soft-sighing breezes, like wayfarers to death, staggered the two men, the woman, and the huskies.

With the dogs falling, Mercedes weeping and riding, Hal swearing innocuously, and Charles's eyes wistfully watering, they staggered into John

Thornton's camp at the mouth of White River. When they halted, the dogs dropped down as though they had all been struck dead. Mercedes dried her eyes and looked at John Thornton. Charles sat down on a log to rest. He sat down very slowly and painstakingly aware of his great stiffness. Hal did the talking. John Thornton was whittling the last touches on an ax handle he had made from a stick of birch. He whittled and listened, gave monosyllabic replies, and, when it was asked, terse advice. He knew the breed, and he gave his advice in the certainty that it would not be followed.

"They told us up above that the bottom was dropping out of the trail and that the best thing for us to do was to lay over," Hal said in response to Thornton's warning to take no more chances on the rotten ice. "They told us we couldn't make White River, and here we are." This last with a sneering ring of triumph in it.

"And they told you true," John Thornton answered. "The bottom's likely to drop out at any moment. Only fools, with the blind luck of fools, could have made it. I tell you straight, I wouldn't risk my carcass on that ice for all the gold in Alaska."

"That's because you're not a fool, I suppose," said Hal. "All the same, we'll go on to Dawson." He uncoiled his whip. "Get up there, Buck! Hi! Get up there! Mush on!"

Thornton went on whittling. It was idle, he knew, to get between a fool and his folly; while two or three fools more or less would not alter the scheme of things.

But the team did not get up at the command. It had long since passed into the stage where blows were required to rouse it. The whip flashed out, here and there, on its merciless errands. John Thornton compressed his lips. Sol-leks was the first to crawl to his feet. Teek followed. Joe came next, yelping with pain. Pike made painful efforts. Twice he fell over, when half up, and on the third attempt managed to rise. Buck made no effort. He lay quietly where he had fallen. The lash bit into him again and again, but he neither whined nor struggled. Several times Thornton started, as though to speak, but changed his mind. A moisture came into his eyes, and, as the whipping continued, he arose and walked irresolutely up and down.

This was the first time Buck had failed, in itself a sufficient reason to drive Hal into a rage. He exchanged the whip for the customary club. Buck refused to move under the rain of heavier blows which now fell upon him. Like his mates, he was barely able to get up, but, unlike them, he had made up his mind not to get up. He had a vague feeling of impending doom. This had been strong upon him when he pulled in to the bank, and it had not departed from him. What with the thin and rotten ice he had felt under his feet all day, it seemed that he sensed disaster close at hand, out there ahead on the ice where his master was trying to drive him. He refused to stir. So greatly had he suffered, and so far gone was he, that the blows did not hurt much. And as they continued to fall upon him, the spark of life within flickered and went down. It was nearly out. He felt strangely numb. As though from a great distance, he was aware that he was being beaten. The last sensations of pain left him. He no longer felt anything, though very faintly he could hear the impact of the club upon his body. But it was no longer his body, it seemed so far away.

And then, suddenly, without warning, uttering a cry that was inarticulate and more like the cry of an animal, John Thornton sprang upon the man who wielded the club. Hal was hurled backward, as though struck by a falling tree. Mercedes screamed. Charles looked on wistfully, wiped his watery eyes, but did not get up because of his stiffness.

John Thornton stood over Buck, struggling to control himself, too convulsed with rage to speak.

"If you strike that dog again, I'll kill you," he at last managed to say in a choking voice.

"It's my dog," Hal replied, wiping the blood from his mouth as he came back. "Get out of my way, or I'll fix you. I'm going to Dawson."

Thornton stood between him and Buck, and evinced no intention of getting out of the way. Hal drew his long hunting knife. Mercedes screamed, cried, laughed, and manifested the chaotic abandonment of hysteria. Thornton rapped Hal's knuckles with the ax handle, knocking the knife to the ground. He rapped his knuckles again as he tried to pick it up. Then he stooped, picked it up himself, and with two strokes cut Buck's traces.

Hal had no fight left in him. Besides, his hands were full with his sister, or his arms, rather; while Buck was too near dead to be of further use in hauling the sled. A few minutes later they pulled out from the bank and down the river. Buck heard them go and raised his head to see. Pike was leading, Sol-leks was at the wheel, and between were Joe and Teek. They were limping and staggering. Mercedes was riding the loaded sled. Hal guided at the gee pole, and Charles stumbled along in the rear.

As Buck watched them, Thornton knelt beside him and with rough, kindly hands searched for broken bones. By the time his search had disclosed nothing more than many bruises and a state of terrible starvation, the sled was a quarter of a mile away.

Dog and man watched it crawling along over the ice. Suddenly, they saw its back end drop down, as into a rut, and the gee pole, with Hal clinging to it, jerk into the air. Mercedes's scream came to their ears. They saw Charles turn and make one step to run back, and then a whole section of ice give way and dogs and humans disappear. A yawning hole was all that was to be seen. The bottom had dropped out of the trail.

John Thornton and Buck looked at each other.

"You poor devil," said John Thornton, and Buck licked his hand.

Chapter 

For the Love of a Man

WHEN JOHN THORNTON froze his feet in the previous December, his partners had made him comfortable and left him to get well, going on themselves up the river to get out a raft of saw logs for Dawson. He was still limping slightly at the time he rescued Buck, but with the continued warm weather even the slight limp left him. And here, lying by the river bank through the long spring days, watching the running water, listening lazily to the songs of birds and the hum of nature, Buck slowly won back his strength.

A rest comes very good after one has traveled three thousand miles, and it must be confessed that Buck waxed lazy as his wounds healed, his muscles swelled out, and the flesh came back to cover his bones. For that matter, they were all loafing—Buck, John Thornton, and Skeet and Nig—waiting for the raft to come that was to carry them down to Dawson. Skeet was a little Irish setter who early made friends with Buck, who, in a dying condition, was unable to resent her first advances. She had the doctor trait which some dogs possess; and as a mother cat washes her kittens, so she washed and cleansed Buck's wounds. Regularly, each morning after he had finished his breakfast, she performed her self-appointed task, till he came to look for her ministrations as much as he did for Thornton's. Nig, equally friendly, though less demonstrative, was a huge black dog, half bloodhound and half deerhound, with eyes that laughed and a boundless good nature.

To Buck's surprise these dogs manifested no jealousy toward him. They seemed to share the kindliness and largeness of John Thornton. As Buck grew stronger they enticed him into all sorts of ridiculous games, in which Thornton himself could not forbear to join; and in this fashion Buck romped through his convalescence and into a new existence. Love, genuine passionate love, was his for the first time. This he had never experienced at Judge Miller's down in the sun-kissed Santa Clara Valley. With the Judge's sons, hunting and tramping, it had been a working partnership; with the Judge's grandsons, a sort of pompous guardianship; and with the Judge himself, a stately and dignified friendship. But love that was feverish and burning, that was adoration, that was madness, it had taken John Thornton to arouse.

This man had saved his life, which was something; but, further, he was the ideal master. Other men saw to the welfare of their dogs from a sense of duty and business expediency; he saw to the welfare of his as if they were his own children, because he could not help it. And he saw further. He never forgot a kindly greeting or a cheering word, and to sit down for a long talk with them (gas, he called it) was as much his delight as theirs. He had a way of taking Buck's head roughly between his hands, and resting his own head upon Buck's, of shaking him back and forth, the while calling him ill names that to Buck were love names. Buck knew no greater joy than that rough embrace and the sound of murmured oaths, and at each jerk back and forth it seemed that his heart would be shaken out of his body so great was its ecstasy. And when, released, he sprang to his feet, his mouth laughing, his eyes eloquent, his throat vibrant with unuttered sound, and in that fashion remained without movement, John Thornton would reverently exclaim, "God! you can all but speak!"

Buck had a trick of love expression that was akin to hurt. He would often seize Thornton's hand in his mouth and close so fiercely that the flesh bore the impress of his teeth for some time afterward. And as Buck understood the oaths to be love words, so the man understood this feigned bite for a caress.

For the most part, however, Buck's love was expressed in adoration. While he went wild with happiness when Thornton touched him or spoke to him, he did not seek these tokens. Unlike Skeet, who was wont to shove her nose under Thornton's hand and nudge and nudge till petted, or Nig, who would stalk up and rest his great head on Thornton's knee, Buck was content to adore at a distance. He would lie by the hour, eager, alert, at Thornton's feet, looking up into his face, dwelling upon it, studying it, following with keenest interest each fleeting expression, every movement or change of feature. Or, as chance might have it, he would lie farther away, to the side or rear, watching the outlines of the man and the occasional movements of his body. And often, such was the communion in which they lived, the strength of Buck's gaze would draw John Thornton's head around, and he would return the gaze, without speech, his heart shining out of his eyes as Buck's heart shone out.

For a long time after his rescue, Buck did not like Thornton to get out of his sight. From the moment he left the tent to when he entered it again, Buck would follow at his heels. His transient masters since he had come into the Northland had bred in him a fear that no master could be permanent. He was afraid that Thornton would pass out of his life as Perrault and François and and the Scotch half-breed had passed out. Even in the night, in his dreams, he was haunted by this fear. At such times he would shake off sleep and creep through the chill to the flap of the tent, where he would stand and listen to the sound of his master's breathing.

But in spite of this great love he bore John Thornton, which seemed to bespeak the soft, civilizing influence; the strain of the primitive, which the Northland had aroused in him, remained alive and active. Faithfulness and devotion, things born of fire and roof, were his; yet he retained his wildness and wiliness. He was a thing of the wild, come in from the wild to sit by John Thornton's fire, rather than a dog of the soft Southland stamped with the marks of generations of civilization. Because of his very great love, he could not steal from this man, but from any other man, in any other camp, he did not hesitate an instant; while the cunning with which he stole enabled him to escape detection.

His face and body were scored by the teeth of many dogs, and he fought as fiercely as ever and more shrewdly. Skeet and Nig were too good-natured for quarreling—besides, they belonged to John Thornton; but the strange dog, no matter what the breed or valor, swiftly acknowledged Buck's supremacy or found himself struggling for life with a terrible antagonist. And Buck was merciless. He had learned well the law of club and fang, and he never forwent an advantage or drew back from a foe he had started on the way to Death. He had lessoned from Spitz, and from the chief fighting dogs of the police and mail, and knew there was no middle course. He must master or be mastered; while to show mercy was a weakness. Mercy did not exist in the primordial life. It was misunderstood for fear, and such misunderstandings made for death. Kill or be killed, eat or be eaten, was the law; and this mandate, down out of the depths of Time, he obeyed.

He was older than the days he had seen and the breaths he had drawn. He linked the past with the present, and the eternity behind him throbbed through him in a mighty rhythm to which he swayed as the tides and seasons swayed. He sat by John Thornton's fire, a broad-breasted dog, white-fanged and long-furred; but behind him were the shades of all manner of dogs, half wolves and wild wolves, urgent and prompting, tasting the savor of the meat he ate, thirsting for the water he drank, scenting the wind with him, listening with him and telling him the sounds made by the wild life in the forest, dictating his moods, directing his actions, lying down to sleep with him when he lay down, and dreaming with him and beyond him and becoming themselves the stuff of his dreams.

So peremptorily did these shades beckon him, that each day mankind and the claims of mankind slipped farther from him. Deep in the forest a call was sounding, and as often as he heard this call, mysteriously thrilling and luring, he felt compelled to turn his back upon the fire and the beaten earth around it, and to plunge into the forest, and on and on, he knew not where or why; nor did he wonder where or why, the call sounding imperiously, deep in the forest. But as often as he gained the soft unbroken earth and the green shade, the love for John Thornton drew him back to the fire again.

Thornton alone held him. The rest of mankind was as nothing. Chance travelers might praise or pet him; but he was cold under it all, and from a too demonstrative man he would get up and walk away. When Thornton's partners, Hans and Pete, arrived on the long-expected raft, Buck refused to notice them till he learned they were close to Thornton; after that he tolerated them in a passive sort of way, accepting favors from them as though he favored them by accepting. They were of the same large type as Thornton, living close to the earth, thinking simply and seeing clearly; and ere they swung the raft into the big eddy by the sawmill at Dawson, they understood Buck and his ways, and did not insist upon an intimacy such as obtained with Skeet and Nig.

For Thornton, however, his love seemed to grow and grow. He, alone among men, could put a pack upon Buck's back in the summer traveling. Nothing was too great for Buck to do, when Thornton commanded. One day (they had grubstaked themselves from the proceeds of the raft and left Dawson for the headwaters of the Tanana) the men and dogs were sitting on the crest of a cliff which fell away, straight down, to naked bedrock three hundred feet below. John Thornton was sitting near the edge, Buck at his shoulder. A thoughtless whim seized Thornton, and he drew the attention of Hans and Pete to the experiment he had in mind. "Jump, Buck!" he commanded, sweeping his arm out and over the chasm. The next instant he was grappling with Buck on the extreme edge, while Hans and Pete were dragging them back into safety.

"It's uncanny," Pete said, after it was over and they had caught their speech.

Thornton shook his head. "No, it is splendid, and it is terrible, too. Do you know, it sometimes makes me afraid."

"I'm not hankering to be the man that lays hands on you while he's around," Pete announced conclusively, nodding his head toward Buck.

"Py Jingo!" was Hans's contribution. "Not mineself either."

It was at Circle City, ere the year was out, that Pete's apprehensions were realized. "Black" Burton, a man evil-tempered and malicious, had been picking a quarrel with a tenderfoot at the bar, when Thornton stepped good-naturedly between. Buck, as was his custom, was lying in a corner, head on paws, watching his master's every action. Burton struck out, without warning, straight from the shoulder. Thornton was sent spinning, and saved himself from falling only by clutching the rail of the bar.

Those who were looking on heard what was neither bark nor yelp, but a something which is best described as a roar, and they saw Buck's body rise up in the air as he left the floor for Burton's throat. The man saved his life by instinctively throwing out his arm, but was hurled backward to the floor with Buck on top of him. Buck loosed his teeth from the flesh of the arm and drove in again for the throat. This time the man succeeded only in partly blocking, and his throat was torn open. Then the crowd was upon Buck, and he was driven off; but while a surgeon checked the bleeding he prowled up and down, growling furiously, attempting to rush in, and being forced back by an array of hostile clubs. A "miners' meeting," called on the spot, decided that the dog had sufficient provocation, and Buck was discharged. But his reputation was made, and from that day his name spread through every camp in Alaska.

Later on, in the fall of the year, he saved John Thornton's life in quite another fashion. The three partners were lining a long and narrow poling boat down a bad stretch of rapids on the Forty Mile Creek. Hans and Pete moved along the bank, snubbing with a thin Manila rope from tree to tree, while Thornton remained in the boat, helping its descent by means of a pole, and shouting directions to the shore. Buck, on the bank, worried and anxious, kept abreast of the boat, his eyes never off his master.

At a particularly bad spot, where a ledge of barely submerged rocks jutted out into the river, Hans cast off the rope, and, while Thornton poled the boat out into the stream, ran down the bank with the end in his hand to snub the boat when it had cleared the ledge. This it did, and was flying downstream in a current as swift as a millrace, when Hans checked it with the rope and checked too suddenly. The boat flirted over and snubbed in to the bank bottom up, while Thornton, flung sheer out of it, was carried downstream toward the worst part of the rapids, a stretch of wild water in which no swimmer could live.

Buck had sprung in on the instant; and at the end of three hundred yards, amid a mad swirl of water, he overhauled Thornton. When he felt him grasp his tail, Buck headed for the bank, swimming with all his splendid strength. But the progress shoreward was slow, the progress downstream amazingly rapid. From below came the fatal roaring where the wild current went wilder and was rent in shreds and spray by the rocks which thrust through like the teeth of an enormous comb. The suck of the water as it took the beginning of the last steep pitch was frightful, and Thornton knew that the shore was impossible. He scraped furiously over a rock, bruised across a second, and struck a third with crushing force. He clutched its slippery top with both hands, releasing Buck, and above the roar of the churning water shouted: "Go, Buck! Go!"

Buck could not hold his own, and swept on downstream, struggling desperately, but unable to win back. When he heard Thornton's command repeated, he partly reared out of the water, throwing his head high, as though for a last look, then turned obediently toward the bank. He swam powerfully and was dragged ashore by Pete and Hans at the very point where swimming ceased to be possible and destruction began.

They knew that the time a man could cling to a slippery rock in the face of that driving current was a matter of minutes, and they ran as fast as they could up the bank to a point far above where Thornton was hanging on. They attached the line with which they had been snubbing the boat to Buck's neck and shoulders, being careful that it should neither strangle him nor impede his swimming, and launched him into the stream. He struck out boldly, but not straight enough into the stream. He discovered the mistake too late, when Thornton was abreast of him and a bare half-dozen strokes away while he was being carried helplessly past.

Hans promptly snubbed with the rope, as though Buck were a boat. The rope thus tightening on him in the sweep of the current, he was jerked under the surface, and under the surface he remained till his body struck against the bank and he was hauled out. He was half drowned, and Hans and Pete threw themselves upon him, pounding the breath into him and the water out of him. He staggered to his feet and fell down. The faint sound of Thornton's voice came to them, and though they could not make out the words of it, they knew that he was in his extremity. His master's voice acted on Buck like an electric shock. He sprang to his feet and ran up the bank ahead of the men to the point of his previous departure.

Again the rope was attached and he was launched, and again he struck out, but this time straight into the stream. He had miscalculated once, but he would not be guilty of it a second time. Hans paid out the rope, permitting no slack, while Pete kept it clear of coils. Buck held on till he was on a line straight above Thornton; then he turned, and with the speed of an express train headed down upon him. Thornton saw him coming, and, as Buck struck him like a battering ram, with the whole force of the current behind him, he reached up and closed with both arms around the shaggy neck. Hans snubbed the rope around the tree, and Buck and Thornton were jerked under the water. Strangling, suffocating, sometimes one uppermost and sometimes the other, dragging over the jagged bottom, smashing against rocks and snags, they veered in to the bank.

Thornton came to, belly downward and being violently propelled back and forth across a drift log by Hans and Pete. His first glance was for Buck, over whose limp and apparently lifeless body Nig was setting up a howl, while Skeet was licking the wet face and closed eyes. Thornton was himself bruised and battered, and he went carefully over Buck's body, when he had been brought around, finding three broken ribs.

"That settles it," he announced. "We camp right here." And camp they did, till Buck's ribs knitted and he was able to travel.

That winter, at Dawson, Buck performed another exploit, not so heroic, perhaps, but one that put his name many notches higher on the totem pole of Alaskan fame. This exploit was particularly gratifying to the three men; for they stood in need of the outfit which it furnished, and were enabled to make a long-desired trip into the virgin East, where miners had not yet appeared. It was brought about by a conversation in the Eldorado Saloon, in which men waxed boastful of their favorite dogs. Buck, because of his record, was the target for these men, and Thornton was driven stoutly to defend him. At the end of half an hour one man stated that his dog could start a sled with five hundred pounds and walk off with it; a second bragged six hundred for his dog; and a third, seven hundred.

"Pooh! pooh! said John Thornton; "Buck can start a thousand pounds."

"And break it out! and walk off with it for a hundred yards?" demanded Matthewson, a Bonanza King, he of the seven hundred vaunt.

"And break it out, and walk off with it for a hundred yards," John Thornton said coolly.

"Well," Matthewson said, slowly and deliberately, so that all could hear, "I've got a thousand dollars that says he can't. And there it is." So saying, he slammed a sack of gold dust of the size of a bologna sausage down upon the bar.

Nobody spoke. Thornton's bluff, if bluff it was, had been called. He could feel a flush of warm blood creeping up his face. His tongue had tricked him. He did not know whether Buck could start a thousand pounds. Half a ton! The enormousness of it appalled him. He had great faith in Buck's strength and had often thought him capable of starting such a load; but never, as now, had he faced the possibility of it, the eyes of a dozen men fixed upon him, silent and waiting. Further, he had no thousand dollars; nor had Hans or Pete.

"I've got a sled standing outside now, with twenty fifty-pound sacks of flour on it," Matthewson went on with brutal directness; "so don't let that hinder you."

Thornton did not reply. He did not know what to say. He glanced from face to face in the absent way of a man who has lost the power of thought and is seeking somewhere to find the thing that will start it going again. The face of Jim O'Brien, a Mastodon King and old-time comrade, caught his eyes. It was as a cue to him, seeming to rouse him to do what he would never have dreamed of doing.

"Can you lend me a thousand?" he asked, almost in a whisper.

"Sure," answered O'Brien, thumping down a plethoric sack by the side of Matthewson's. "Though it's little faith I'm having, John, that the beast can do the trick."

The Eldorado emptied its occupants into the street to see the test. The tables were deserted, and the dealers and gamekeepers came forth to see the outcome of the wager and to lay odds. Several hundred men, furred and mittened, banked around the sled within easy distance. Matthewson's sled, loaded with a thousand pounds of flour, had been standing for a couple of hours, and in the intense cold (it was sixty below zero) the runners had frozen fast to the hard-packed snow. Men offered odds of two to one that Buck could not budge the sled. A quibble arose concerning the phrase "break out." O'Brien contended it was Thornton's privilege to knock the runners loose, leaving Buck to "break it out" from a dead standstill. Matthewson insisted that the phrase included breaking the runners from the frozen grip of the snow. A majority of the men who had witnessed the making of the bet decided in his favor, whereat the odds went up to three to one against Buck.

There were no takers. Not a man believed him capable of the feat. Thornton had been hurried into the wager, heavy with doubt; and now that he looked at the sled itself, the concrete fact, with the regular team of ten dogs curled up in the snow before it, the more impossible the task appeared. Matthewson waxed jubilant.

"Three to one!" he proclaimed. "I'll lay you another thousand at that figure, Thornton. What d'ye say?"

Thornton's doubt was strong in his face, but his fighting spirit was aroused—the fighting spirit that soars above odds, fails to recognize the impossible, and is deaf to all save the clamor for battle. He called Hans and Pete to him. Their sacks were slim, and with his own, the three partners could rake together only two hundred dollars. In the ebb of their fortunes, this sum was their total capital; yet they laid it unhesitatingly against Matthewson's six hundred.

The team of ten dogs was unhitched, and Buck, with his own harness, was put into the sled. He had caught the contagion of the excitement, and he felt that in some way he must do a great thing for John Thornton. Murmurs of admiration at his splendid appearance went up. He was in perfect condition, without an ounce of superfluous flesh, and the one hundred and fifty pounds that he weighed were so many pounds of grit and virility. His furry coat shone with the sheen of silk. Down the neck and across the shoulders, his mane, in repose as it was, half bristled and seemed to lift with every movement, as though excess of vigor made each particular hair alive and active. The great breast and heavy forelegs were no more than in proportion with the rest of the body, where the muscles showed in tight rolls underneath the skin. Men felt these muscles and proclaimed them hard as iron, and the odds went down to two to one.

"Gad, sir! Gad, sir!" stuttered a member of the latest dynasty, a king of the Skookum Benches. "I offer you eight hundred for him, sir, before the test, sir; eight hundred just as he stands."

Thornton shook his head and stepped to Buck's side.

"You must stand off from him," Matthewson protested. "Free play and plenty of room."

The crowd fell silent; only could be heard the voices of the gamblers vainly offering two to one. Everybody acknowledged Buck a magnificent animal, but twenty fifty-pound sacks of flour bulked too large in their eyes for them to loosen their pouch strings.

Thornton knelt down by Buck's side. He took his head in his two hands and rested cheek to cheek. He did not playfully shake him, as was his wont, or murmur soft love curses; but he whispered in his ear. "As you love me, Buck. As you love me," was what he whispered. Buck whined with suppressed eagerness.

The crowd was watching curiously. The affair was growing mysterious. It seemed like a conjuration. As Thornton got to his feet, Buck seized his mittened hand between his jaws, pressing in with his teeth and releasing slowly, half-reluctantly. It was the answer, in terms, not of speech, but of love. Thornton stepped well back.

"Now, Buck," he said.

Buck tightened the traces, then slacked them for a matter of several inches. It was the way he had learned.

"Gee!" Thornton's voice rang out, sharp in the tense silence.

Buck swung to the right, ending the movement in a plunge that took up the slack and with a sudden jerk arrested his one hundred and fifty pounds. The load quivered, and from under the runners arose a crisp crackling.

"Haw!" Thornton commanded.

Buck duplicated the maneuver, this time to the left. The crackling turned into a snapping, the sled pivoting and the runners slipping and grating several inches to the side. The sled was broken out. Men were holding their breaths, intensely unconscious of the fact.

"Now, MUSH!"

Thornton's command cracked out like a pistol shot. Buck threw himself forward, tightening the traces with a jarring lunge. His whole body was gathered compactly together in the tremendous effort, the muscles writhing and knotting like live things under the silky fur. His great chest was low to the ground, his head forward and down, while his feet were flying like mad, the claws scarring the hard-packed snow in parallel grooves. The sled swayed and trembled, half-started forward. One of his feet slipped, and one man groaned aloud. Then the sled lurched ahead in what appeared a rapid succession of jerks, though it never really came to a dead stop again

. . . half an inch . . . an inch . . . two inches. . . . The jerks perceptibly diminished; as the sled gained momentum, he caught them up, till it was moving steadily along.

Men gasped and began to breathe again, unaware that for a moment they had ceased to breathe. Thornton was running behind, encouraging Buck with short, cheery words. The distance had been measured off, and as he neared the pile of firewood which marked the end of the hundred yards, a cheer began to grow and grow, which burst into a roar as he passed the firewood and halted at command. Every man was tearing himself loose, even Mathewson. Hats and mittens were flying in the air. Men were shaking hands, it did not matter with whom, and bubbling over in a general incoherent babel.

But Thornton fell on his knees beside Buck. Head was against head, and he was shaking him back and forth. Those who hurried up heard him cursing Buck, and he cursed him long and fervently, and softly and lovingly.

"Gad, sir! Gad, sir!" spluttered the Skookum Bench king. "I'll give you a thousand for him, sir, a thousand, sir—twelve hundred, sir."

Thornton rose to his feet. His eyes were wet. The tears were streaming frankly down his cheeks. "Sir," he said to the Skookum Bench king, "no, sir. You can go to hell, sir. It's the best I can do for you, sir."

Buck seized Thornton's hand in his teeth. Thornton shook him back and forth. As though animated by a common impulse, the onlookers drew back to a respectful distance; nor were they again indiscreet enough to interrupt.

Chapter 7

The Sounding of the Call

WHEN BUCK EARNED sixteen hundred dollars in five minutes for John Thornton, he made it possible for his master to pay off certain debts and to journey with his partners into the East after a fabled lost mine, the history of which was as old as the history of the country. Many men had sought it; few had found it; and more than a few there were who had never returned from the quest. This lost mine was steeped in tragedy and shrouded in mystery. No one knew of the first man. The oldest tradition stopped before it got back to him. From the beginning there had been an ancient and ramshackle cabin. Dying men had sworn to it, and to the mine the site of which it marked, clinching their testimony with nuggets that were unlike any known grade of gold in the Northland.

But no living man had looted this treasure house, and the dead were dead; wherefore John Thornton and Pete and Hans, with Buck and half a dozen other dogs, faced into the East on an unknown trail to achieve where men and dogs as good as themselves had failed. They sledded seventy miles up the Yukon, swung to the left into the Stewart River, passed the Mayo and the McQuestion, and held on until the Stewart itself became a streamlet, threading the upstanding peaks which marked the backbone of the continent.

John Thornton asked little of man or nature. He was unafraid of the wild. With a handful of salt and a rifle he could plunge into the wilderness and fare wherever he pleased and as long as he pleased. Being in no haste, Indian fashion, he hunted his dinner in the course of the day's travel; and if he failed to find it, like the Indian, he kept on traveling, secure in the knowledge that sooner or later he would come to it. So, on this great journey into the East, straight meat was the bill of fare, ammunition and tools principally made up the load on the sled, and the time card was drawn upon the limitless future.

To Buck it was boundless delight, this hunting, fishing, and indefinite wandering through strange places. For weeks at a time they would hold on steadily, day after day; and for weeks upon end they would camp, here and there, the dogs loafing and the men burning holes through frozen muck and gravel and washing countless pans of dirt by the heat of the fire. Sometimes they went hungry, sometimes they feasted riotously, all according to the abundance of game and the fortune of hunting. Summer arrived, and dogs and men packed on their backs, rafted across blue mountain lakes, and descended or ascended unknown rivers in slender boats whipsawed from the standing forest.

The months came and went, and back and forth they twisted through the uncharted vastness, where no men were and yet where men had been if the Lost Cabin were true. They went across divides in summer blizzards, shivered under the midnight sun on naked mountains between the timber line and the eternal snows, dropped into summer valleys amid swarming gnats and flies, and in the shadows of glaciers picked strawberries and flowers as ripe and fair as any the Southland could boast. In the fall of the year they penetrated a weird lake country, sad and silent, where wild fowl had been, but where then there was no life nor sign of life—only the blowing of chill winds, the forming of ice in sheltered places, and the melancholy rippling of waves on lonely beaches.

And through another winter they wandered on the obliterated trails of men who had gone before. Once, they came upon a path blazed through the forest, an ancient path, and the Lost Cabin seemed very near. But the path began nowhere and ended nowhere, and it remained mystery, as the man who made it and the reason he made it remained mystery. Another time they chanced upon the time-graven wreckage of a hunting lodge, and amid the shreds of rotted blankets John Thornton found a long-barreled flintlock. He knew it for a Hudson Bay Company gun of the young days in the Northwest, when such a gun was worth its height in beaver skins packed flat. And that was all—no hint as to the man who in an early day had reared the lodge and left the gun among the blankets.

Spring came on once more, and at the end of all their wandering they found, not the Lost Cabin, but a shallow placer in a broad valley where the gold showed like yellow butter across the bottom of the washing pan. They sought no farther. Each day they worked earned them thousands of dollars in clean dust and nuggets, and they worked every day. The gold was sacked in moose-hide bags, fifty pounds to the bag, and piled like so much firewood outside the spruce-bough lodge. Like giants they toiled, days flashing on the heels of days like dreams as they heaped the treasure up.

There was nothing for the dogs to do, save the hauling in of meat now and again that Thornton killed, and Buck spent long hours musing by the fire. The vision of the short-legged hairy man came to him more frequently, now that there was little work to be done; and often, blinking by the fire, Buck wandered with him in that other world which he remembered.

The salient thing of this other world seemed fear. When he watched the hairy man sleeping by the fire, head between his knees and hands clasped above, Buck saw that he slept restlessly, with many starts and awakenings, at which times he would peer fearfully into the darkness and fling more wood upon the fire. Did they walk by the beach of a sea, where the hairy man gathered shellfish and ate them as he gathered, it was with eyes that roved everywhere for hidden danger and with legs prepared to run like the wind at its first appearance. Through the forest they crept noiselessly, Buck at the hairy man's heels; and they were alert and vigilant, the pair of them, ears twitching and moving and nostrils quivering, for the man heard and smelled as keenly as Buck. The hairy man could spring up into the trees and travel ahead as fast as on the ground, swinging by the arms from limb to limb, sometimes a dozen feet apart, letting go and catching, never falling, never missing his grip. In fact, he seemed as much at home among the trees as on the ground; and Buck had memories of nights of vigil spent beneath trees wherein the hairy man roosted, holding on tightly as he slept.

And closely akin to the visions of the hairy man

was the call still sounding in the depths of the forest. It filled him with a great unrest and strange desires. It caused him to feel a vague, sweet gladness, and he was aware of wild yearnings and stirrings for he knew not what. Sometimes he pursued the call into the forest, looking for it as though it were a tangible thing, barking softly or defiantly, as the mood might dictate. He would thrust his nose into the cool wood moss, or into the black soil where long grasses grew, and snort with joy at the fat earth smells; or he would crouch for hours, as if in concealment, behind fungus-covered trunks of fallen trees, wide-eyed and wide-eared to all that moved and sounded about him. It might be, lying thus, that he hoped to surprise this call he could not understand. But he did not know why he did these various things. He was impelled to do them, and did not reason about them at all.

Irresistible impulses seized him. He would be lying in camp, dozing lazily in the heat of the day, when suddenly his head would lift and his ears cock up, intent and listening, and he would spring to his feet and dash away, and on and on, for hours, through the forest aisles and across the open spaces where the niggerheads bunched. He loved to run down dry watercourses, and to creep and spy upon the bird life in the woods. For a day at a time he would lie in the underbrush where he could watch the partridges drumming and strutting up and down. But especially he loved to run in the dim twilight of the summer midnights, listening to the subdued and sleepy murmurs of the forest reading signs and sounds as man may read a book, and seeking for the mysterious something that called—called, waking or sleeping, at all times, for him to come.

One night he sprang from sleep with a start, eager-eyed, nostrils quivering and scenting, his mane bristling in recurrent waves. From the forest came the call (or one note of it, for the call was many-noted), distinct and definite as never before—a long-drawn howl, like, yet unlike, any noise made by husky dog. And he knew it, in the old familiar way, as a sound heard before. He sprang through the sleeping camp and in swift silence dashed through the woods. As he drew closer to the cry he went more slowly, with caution in every movement, till he came to an open place among the trees, and looking out saw, erect on haunches, with nose pointed to the sky, a long, lean timber wolf.

He had made no noise, yet it ceased from its howling and tried to sense his presence. Buck stalked into the open, half-crouching, body gathered compactly together, tail straight and stiff, feet falling with unwonted care. Every movement advertised commingled threatening and overture of friendliness. It was the menacing truce that marks the meeting of wild beasts that prey. But the wolf fled at sight of him. He followed, with wild leapings, in a frenzy to overtake. He ran him into a blind channel, in the bed of the creek, where a timber jam barred the way. The wolf whirled about, pivoting on his hind legs after the fashion of Joe and of all cornered husky dogs, snarling and bristling, clipping his teeth together in a continuous and rapid succession of snaps.

Buck did not attack, but circled him about and hedged him in with friendly advances. The wolf was suspicious and afraid; for Buck made three of him in weight, while his head barely reached Buck's shoulder. Watching his chance, he darted away, and the chase was resumed. Time and again he was cornered, and the thing repeated, though he was in poor condition, or Buck could not so easily have overtaken him. He would run till Buck's head was even with his flank, when he would whirl around at bay, only to dash away again at the first opportunity.

But in the end Buck's pertinacity was rewarded; for the wolf, finding that no harm was intended, finally sniffed noses with him. Then they became friendly, and played about in the nervous, half-coy way with which fierce beasts belie their fierceness. After some time of this the wolf started off at an easy lope in a manner that plainly showed he was going somewhere. He made it clear to Buck that he was to come, and they ran side by side through the somber twilight, straight up the creek bed, into the gorge from which it issued, and across the bleak divide where it took its rise.

On the opposite slope of the watershed they came down into a level country where were great stretches of forest and many streams, and through these great stretches they ran steadily, hour after hour, the sun rising higher and the day growing warmer. Buck was wildly glad. He knew he was at last answering the call running by the side of his wood brother toward the place from where the call surely came. Old memories were coming upon him fast, and he was stirring to them as of old he stirred to the realities of which they were the shadows. He had done this thing before, somewhere in that other and dimly remembered world, and he was doing it again, now, running free in the open, the unpacked earth underfoot, the wide sky overhead.

They stopped by a running stream to drink, and, stopping, Buck remembered John Thornton. He sat down. The wolf started on toward the place from where the call surely came, then returned to him, sniffing noses and making actions as though to encourage him. But Buck turned about and started slowly on the back track. For the better part of an hour the wild brother ran by his side, whining softly. Then he sat down, pointed his nose upward, and howled. It was a mournful howl, and as Buck held steadily on his way he heard it grow faint and fainter until it was lost in the distance.

John Thornton was eating dinner when Buck dashed into camp and sprang upon him in a frenzy of affection, overturning him, scrambling upon him, licking his face, biting his hand—"playing the general tomfool," as John Thornton characterized it, the while he shook Buck back and forth and cursed him lovingly.

For two days and nights Buck never left camp, never let Thornton out of his sight. He followed him about at his work, watched him while he ate, saw him into his blankets at night and out of them in the morning. But after two days the call in the forest began to sound more imperiously than ever. Buck's restlessness came back on him, and he was haunted by recollections of the wild brother, and of the smiling land beyond the divide and the run side by side through the wide forest stretches. Once again he took to wandering in the woods, but the wild brother came no more; and though he listened through long vigils, the mournful howl was never raised.

He began to sleep out at night, staying away from camp for days at a time; and once he crossed the divide at the head of the creek and went down into the land of timber and streams. There he wandered for a week, seeking vainly for fresh sign of the wild brother, killing his meat as he traveled and traveling with the long, easy lope that seems never to tire. He fished for salmon in a broad stream that emptied somewhere into the sea, and by this stream he killed a large black bear, blinded by the mosquitoes while likewise fishing, and raging through the forest helpless and terrible. Even so, it was a hard fight, and it aroused the last latent remnants of Buck's ferocity. And two days later, when he returned to his kill and found a dozen wolverines quarreling over the spoil, he scattered them like chaff; and those that fled left two behind who would quarrel no more.

The blood longing became stronger than ever before. He was a killer, a thing that preyed, living on the things that lived, unaided, alone, by virtue of his own strength and prowess, surviving triumphantly in a hostile environment where only the strong survived. Because of all this he became possessed of a great pride in himself, which communicated itself like a contagion to his physical being. It advertised itself in all his movements, was apparent in the play of every muscle, spoke plainly as speech in the way he carried himself, and made his glorious furry coat if anything more glorious. But for the stray brown on his muzzle and above his eyes, and for the splash of white hair that ran midmost down his chest, he might well have been mistaken for a gigantic wolf, larger than the largest of the breed. From his St. Bernard father he had inherited size and weight, but it was his shepherd mother who had given shape to that size and weight. His muzzle was the long wolf muzzle, save that it was larger than the muzzle of any wolf; and his head, somewhat broader, was the wolf head on a massive scale.

His cunning was wolf cunning, and wild cunning; his intelligence, shepherd intelligence and St. Bernard intelligence; and all this, plus an experience gained in the fiercest of schools, made him as formidable a creature as any that roamed the wild. A carnivorous animal, living on a straight meat diet, he was in full flower, at the high tide of his life, overspilling with vigor and virility. When Thornton passed a caressing hand along his back, a snapping and crackling followed the hand, each hair discharging its pent magnetism at the contact. Every part, brain and body, nerve tissue and fiber, was keyed to the most exquisite pitch; and between all the parts there was a perfect equilibrium or adjustment. To sights and sounds and events which required action, he responded with lightning-like rapidity. Quickly as a husky dog could leap to defend from attack or to attack, he could leap twice as quickly. He saw the movement, or heard sound, and responded in less time than another dog required to compass the mere seeing or hearing. He perceived and determined and responded in the same instant. In point of fact the three actions of perceiving, determining, and responding were sequential; but so infinitesimal were the intervals of time between them that they appeared simultaneous. His muscles were surcharged with vitality, and snapped into play sharply, like steel springs. Life streamed through him in splendid flood, glad and rampant, until it seemed that it would burst him asunder in sheer ecstasy and pour forth generously over the world.

"Never was there such a dog," said John Thornton one day, as the partners watched Buck marching out of camp.

"When he was made, the mold was broke," said Pete.

"Py jingo! I t'ink so mineself," Hans affirmed

They saw him marching out of camp, but they did not see the instant and terrible transformation which took place as soon as he was within the secrecy of the forest. He no longer marched. At once he became a thing of the wild, stealing along softly, cat-footed, a passing shadow that appeared and disappeared among the shadows. He knew how to take advantage of every cover, to crawl on his belly like a snake, and like a snake to leap and strike. He could take a ptarmigan from its nest, kill a rabbit as it slept, and snap in midair the little chipmunks fleeing a second too late for the trees. Fish, in open pools, were not too quick for him; nor were beaver, mending their dams, too wary. He killed to eat, not from wantonness; but he preferred to eat what he killed himself. So a lurking humor ran through his deeds, and it was his delight to steal upon the squirrels, and, when he all but had them, to let them go, chattering in mortal fear to the treetops.

As the fall of the year came on, the moose appeared in greater abundance, moving slowly down to meet the winter in the lower and less rigorous valleys. Buck had already dragged down a stray part-grown calf; but he wished strongly for larger and more formidable quarry, and he came upon it one day on the divide at the head of the creek. A band of twenty moose had crossed over from the land of streams and timber, and chief among them was a great bull. He was in a savage temper, and, standing over six feet from the ground, was as formidable an antagonist as even Buck could desire. Back and forth the bull tossed his great palmated antlers, branching to fourteen points and embracing seven feet within the tips. His small eyes burned with a vicious and bitter light, while he roared with fury at sight of Buck.

From the bull's side, just forward of the flank, protruded a feathered arrow end, which accounted for his savageness. Guided by that instinct which came from the old hunting days of the primordial world, Buck proceeded to cut the bull out from the herd. It was no slight task. He would bark and dance about in front of the bull, just out of reach of the great antlers and of the terrible splay hoofs which could have stamped his life out with a single blow. Unable to turn his back on the fanged danger and go on, the bull would be driven into paroxysms of rage. At such moments he charged Buck, who retreated craftily, luring him on by a simulated inability to escape. But when he was thus separated from his fellows, two or three of the younger bulls would charge back upon Buck and enable the wounded bull to rejoin the herd.

There is a patience of the wild—dogged, tireless, persistent as life itself—that holds motionless for endless hours the spider in its web, the snake in its coils, the panther in its ambuscade; this patience belongs peculiarly to life when it hunts its living food; and it belonged to Buck as he clung to the flank of the herd, retarding its march, irritating the young bulls, worrying the cows with their half-grown calves, and driving the wounded bull mad with helpless rage. For half a day this continued. Buck multiplied himself, attacking from all sides, enveloping the herd in a whirlwind of menace, cutting out his victim as fast as it could rejoin its mates, wearing out the patience of creatures preyed upon, which is a lesser patience than that of creatures preying.

As the day wore along and the sun dropped to its bed in the northwest (the darkness had come back and the fall nights were six hours long), the young bulls retraced their steps more and more reluctantly to the aid of their beset leader. The downcoming winter was harrying them on to the lower levels, and it seemed they could never shake off this tireless creature that held them back. Besides, it was not the life of the herd, or of the young bulls, that was threatened. The life of only one member was demanded, which was a remoter interest than their lives, and in the end they were content to pay the toll.

As twilight fell the old bull stood with lowered head, watching his mates—the cows he had known, the calves he had fathered, the bulls he had mastered—as they shambled on at a rapid pace through the fading light. He could not follow, for before his nose leaped the merciless fanged terror that would not let him go. Three hundredweight more than half a ton he weighed, he had lived a long, strong life, full of fight and struggle, and at the end he faced death at the teeth of a creature whose head did not reach beyond his great knuckled knees.

From then on, night and day, Buck never left his prey, never gave it a moment's rest, never permitted it to browse the leaves of trees or the shoots of young birch and willow. Nor did he give the wounded bull opportunity to slake his burning thirst in the slender trickling streams they crossed. Often, in desperation, he burst into long stretches of flight. At such times Buck did not attempt to stay him, but loped easily at his heels, satisfied with the way the game was played, lying down when the moose stood still, attacking him fiercely when he strove to eat or drink.

The great head drooped more and more under its tree of horns, and the shambling trot grew weak and weaker. He took to standing for long periods, with nose to the ground and dejected ears dropped limply; and Buck found more time in which to get water for himself and in which to rest. At such moments, panting with red lolling tongue and with eyes fixed upon the big bull, it appeared to Buck that a change was coming over the face of things. He could feel a new stir in the land. As the moose were coming into the land, other kinds of life were coming in. Forest and stream and air seemed palpitant with their presence. The news of it was borne in upon him, not by sight, or sound, or smell, but by some other and subtler sense. He heard nothing, saw nothing, yet knew that the land was somehow different; that through it strange things were afoot and ranging; and he resolved to investigate after he had finished the business in hand.

At last, at the end of the fourth day, he pulled the great moose down. For a day and a night he remained by the kill, eating and sleeping, turn and turn about. Then, rested, refreshed and strong, he turned his face toward camp and John Thornton. He broke into the long easy lope, and went on, hour after hour, never at loss for the tangled way, heading straight home through strange country with a certitude of direction that put man and his magnetic needle to shame.

As he held on he became more and more conscious of the new stir in the land. There was life abroad in it different from the life which had been there throughout the summer. No longer was this fact borne in upon him in some subtle, mysterious way. The birds talked of it, the squirrels chattered about it, the very breeze whispered of it. Several times he stopped and drew in the fresh morning air in great sniffs, reading a message which made him leap on with greater speed. He was oppressed with a sense of calamity happening, if it were not calamity already happened; and as he crossed the last watershed and dropped down into the valley toward camp, he proceeded with greater caution.

Three miles away he came upon a fresh trail that sent his neck hair rippling and bristling. It led straight toward camp and John Thornton. Buck hurried on, swiftly and stealthily, every nerve straining and tense, alert to the multitudinous details which told a story—all but the end. His nose gave him a varying description of the passage of the life on the heels of which he was traveling. He remarked the pregnant silence of the forest. The bird life had flitted. The squirrels were in hiding. One only he saw—a sleek gray fellow, flattened against a gray dead limb so that he seemed a part of it, a woody excrescence upon the wood itself.

As Buck slid along with the obscureness of a gliding shadow, his nose was jerked suddenly to the side as though a positive force had gripped and pulled it. He followed the new scent into a thicket and found Nig. He was lying on his side, dead where he had dragged himself, an arrow protruding, head and feathers, from either side of his body.

A hundred yards farther on, Buck came upon one of the sled dogs Thornton had bought in Dawson. This dog was thrashing about in a death struggle, directly on the trail, and Buck passed around him without stopping. From the camp came the faint sound of many voices, rising and falling in a singsong chant. Bellying forward to the edge of the clearing, he found Hans, lying on his face, feathered with arrows like a porcupine. At the same instant Buck peered out where the spruce-bough lodge had been and saw what made his hair leap straight up on his neck and shoulders. A gust of overpowering rage swept over him. He did not know that he growled, but he growled aloud with a terrible ferocity. For the last time in his life he allowed passion to usurp cunning and reason, and it was because of his great love for John Thornton that he lost his head.

The Yeehats were dancing about the wreckage of the spruce-bough lodge when they heard a fearful roaring and saw rushing upon them an animal the like of which they had never seen before. It was Buck, a live hurricane of fury, hurling himself upon them in a frenzy to destroy. He sprang at the foremost man (it was the chief of the Yeehats), ripping the throat wide open till the rent jugular spouted a fountain of blood. He did not pause to worry the victim, but ripped in passing, with the next bound tearing wide the throat of a second man. There was no withstanding him. He plunged about in their very midst, tearing, rending, destroying, in constant and terrific motion which defied the arrows they discharged at him. In fact, so inconceivably rapid were his movements, and so closely were the Indians tangled together, that they shot one another with the arrows; and one young hunter, hurling a spear at Buck in midair, drove it through the chest of another hunter with such force that the point broke through the skin of the back and stood out beyond. Then a panic seized the Yeehats, and they fled in terror to the woods, proclaiming as they fled the advent of the Evil Spirit.

And truly Buck was the Fiend incarnate raging at their heels and dragging them down like deer as they raced through the trees. It was a fateful day for the Yeehats. They scattered far and wide over the country and it was not till a week later that the last of the survivors gathered together in a lower valley and counted their losses. As for Buck, wearying of the pursuit, he returned to the desolated camp. He found Pete where he had been killed in his blankets in the first moment of surprise. Thornton's desperate struggle was fresh-written on the earth, and Buck scented every detail of it down to the edge of a deep pool. By the edge, head and forefeet in the water, lay Skeet, faithful to the last. The pool itself, muddy and discolored from the sluice boxes, effectually hid what it contained, and it contained John Thornton; for Buck followed his trace into the water, from which no trace led away.

All day Buck brooded by the pool or roamed restlessly about the camp. Death, as a cessation of movement, as a passing out and away from the lives of the living, he knew, and he knew John Thornton was dead. It left a great void in him, somewhat akin to hunger, but a void which ached and ached, and which food could not fill. At times, when he paused to contemplate the carcasses of the Yeehats, he forgot the pain of it; and at such times he was aware of a great pride in himself—a pride greater than any he had yet experienced. He had killed man, the noblest game of all, and he had killed in the face of the law of club and fang. He sniffed the bodies curiously. They had died so easily. It was harder to kill a husky dog than them. They were no match at all, were it not for their arrows and spears and clubs. Thenceforward he would be unafraid of them except when they bore in their hands their arrows, spears, and clubs.

Night came on, and a full moon rose high over the trees into the sky, lighting the land till it lay bathed in ghostly day. And with the coming of the night, brooding and mourning by the pool, Buck became alive to a stirring of the new life in the forest other than that which the Yeehats had made. He stood up, listening and scenting. From far away drifted a faint, sharp yelp, followed by a chorus of similar sharp yelps. As the moments passed the yelps grew closer and louder. Again Buck knew them as things heard in that other world which persisted in his memory. He walked to the center of the open space and listened. It was the call, the many-noted call, sounding more luringly and compellingly than ever before. And as never before, he was ready to obey. John Thornton was dead. The last tie was broken. Man and the claims of man no longer bound him.

Hunting their living meat, as the Yeehats were hunting it, on the flanks of the migrating moose, the wolf pack had at last crossed over from the land of streams and timber and invaded Buck's valley. Into the clearing where the moonlight streamed, they poured in a silvery flood; and in the center of the clearing stood Buck, motionless as a statue, waiting their coming. They were awed, so still and large he stood, and a moment's pause fell, till the boldest one leaped straight for him. Like a flash Buck struck, breaking the neck. Then he stood, without movement, as before, the stricken wolf rolling in agony behind him. Three others tried it in sharp succession; and one after the other they drew back, streaming blood from slashed throats or shoulders.

This was sufficient to fling the whole pack forward, pell-mell, crowded together, blocked and confused by its eagerness to pull down the prey. Buck's marvelous quickness and agility stood him in good stead. Pivoting on his hind legs, and snapping and gashing, he was everywhere at once, presenting a front which was apparently unbroken so swiftly did he whirl and guard from side to side. But to prevent them from getting behind him, he was forced back, down past the pool and into the creek bed, till he brought up against a high gravel bank. He worked along to a right angle in the bank which the men had made in the course of mining, and in this angle he came to bay, protected on three sides and with nothing to do but face the front.

And so well did he face it, that at the end of half an hour the wolves drew back discomfited. The tongues of all were out and lolling, the white fangs showing cruelly white in the moonlight. Some were lying down with heads raised and ears pricked forward; others stood on their feet, watching him; and still others were lapping water from the pool. One wolf, long and lean and gray, advanced cautiously, in a friendly manner, and Buck recognized the wild brother with whom he had run for a night and a day. He was whining softly, and, as Buck whined, they touched noses.

Then an old wolf, gaunt and battle-scarred, came forward. Buck writhed his lips into the preliminary of a snarl, but sniffed noses with him. Whereupon the old wolf sat down, pointed nose at the moon, and broke out the long wolf howl. The others sat down and howled. And now the call came to Buck in unmistakable accents. He, too, sat down and howled. This over, he came out of his angle and the pack crowded around him, sniffing in half-friendly, half-savage manner. The leaders lifted the yelp of the pack and sprang away into the woods. The wolves swung in behind, yelping in chorus. And Buck ran with them, side by side with the wild brother, yelping as he ran.

And here may well end the story of Buck. The years were not many when the Yeehats noted a change in the breed of timber wolves; for some were seen with splashes of brown on head and muzzle, and with a rift of white centering down the chest. But more remarkable than this, the Yeehats tell of a Ghost Dog that runs at the head of the pack. They are afraid of this Ghost Dog, for it has cunning greater than they, stealing from their camps in fierce winters, robbing their traps, slaying their dogs, and defying their bravest hunters.

Nay, the tale grows worse. Hunters there are who fail to return to the camp, and hunters there have been whom their tribesmen found with throats slashed cruelly open and with wolf prints about them in the snow greater than the prints of any wolf. Each fall when the Yeehats follow the movement of the moose, there is a certain valley which they never enter. And women there are who become sad when the word goes over the fire of how the Evil Spirit came to select that valley for an abiding place.

In the summers there is one visitor, however, to that valley, of which the Yeehats do not know. It is a great, gloriously coated wolf, like, and yet unlike, all other wolves. He crosses alone from the smiling timber land and comes down into an open space among the trees. Here a yellow stream flows from rotted moose-hide sacks and sinks into the ground, with long grasses growing through it and vegetable mold overrunning it and hiding its yellow from the sun; and here he muses for a time, howling once, long and mournfully, ere he departs.

But he is not always alone. When the long winter nights come on and the wolves follow their meat into the lower valleys, he may be seen running at the head of the pack through the pale moonlight or glimmering borealis, leaping gigantic above his fellows, his great throat a-bellow as he sings a song of the younger world, which is the song of the pack.

Related Readings

The Wolf and the Dog

by Marie de France

In this poem a wolf and a dog contrast their lives. With which character would Buck agree?

A wolf and dog met on the way
While passing through the woods one day.
The wolf looked closely at the dog,
And then began this dialogue:
5 "Brother," he said, "you look so fine!
And oh, such fur! How it does shine!"
The dog replied, "That's very true;
I eat quite well, a great deal, too.
Each day I make my cozy seat
10 While resting at my master's feet
Where daily I gnaw bones, and that
Is what makes me so big and fat.
If you would like to come with me,
If to obey him you'll agree—
15 And act like me—you'll have from this
More food than you could ever wish."
"I'll do that! Sure!" the wolf replied.
Together off they went, allied.
Before they'd at the town arrived,
20 The wolf looked at the dog and eyed
The way the dog a collar wore
And how a dragging chain he bore.
"Brother," he said, "how odd is that
Thing 'round your neck—I know not what."
25 "That's my chain-leash," the dog replied

"with which all through the week I'm tied;
For his possessions I would chew on,
And many items I would ruin.
My master wants them all protected,
30 And that's why I'm tied and restricted.
At night, around the house I peer
And make sure that no thieves draw near."
"What!" cried the wolf. "By this you mean
You can't go out except with him!
35 Well, you can stay! I won't remain.
I'll never choose to wear a chain!
I'd rather live as a wolf, free,
Than on a chain in luxury.
I still can make a choice, and so
40 You fare to town; to woods I'll go."
A chain thus brought the termination
Of friendship and fraternization.

from The Hidden Life of Dogs

by Elizabeth Marshall Thomas

Do you believe that dogs like Buck have thoughts and emotions like humans do? In the introduction to The Hidden Life of Dogs, *Elizabeth Marshall Thomas, an author who has spent years studying dog behavior, defends anthropomorphism—the belief that animals have human-like motivations, characteristics, and behavior.*

. . . While the question of animal consciousness is a perfectly valid field for scientific exploration, the general assumption that other creatures lack consciousness is astonishing.

After all, thoughts and emotions have evolutionary value. If they didn't, we wouldn't have them. Thought is an efficient, effective mechanism that we, and many other animals, would be hard put to do without. With intellect, which is to say the ability to learn and reason, an organism such as a person or a dog can cope with a wide variety of problems that would require an enormous amount of hard-wiring if the behavioral solution to each problem were preprogrammed. When we relegate animal thought to instinct, we overlook the fact that instinct is merely an elegant matrix for the formation of an intellect, a fail-safe device that guides each species to form thoughts. When shaped by education, our thoughts enable us to do what we do, and even to be what we are, not only as members of our species but as individuals.

As for consciousness, consider the four following observations: the first of a dog's custom, the second of a dog weighing two alternatives, the third of a dog playing a game, and the fourth of a dog who figured out and temporarily adopted a human mannerism. The dog's custom was started in a household in Boulder, Colorado, by five dogs who, unlike any other dogs this author has ever seen, ate lying down. They certainly had not been trained to do this—on the contrary, the owners found nothing remarkable about the custom and in fact seemed touchingly unaware that other dogs ate differently. Why did these dogs eat lying down? No one knew for sure. The alpha dog, a male Australian shepherd named Rider, had apparently started the custom, perhaps to reduce excitement and competition at mealtimes, when his owners, busy parents with five children and overloaded schedules, would plunk down five bowls of kibbles in the yard and get on with the next urgent matter. Thus the dogs had to police themselves. Quickly choosing a bowl, each dog would lie down and eat the food. Later, almost as if at a signal, all would get up and move around, licking out one another's dishes. Giving the impression that they considered their behavior perfectly ordinary, the dogs invariably left human observers perplexed.

Yet it is possible to guess at a reason for the custom: Rider is frailer than two of the others, both hefty females with barrel bodies and Percheron hips. One is significantly older than Rider, and both are excitable when mealtimes come. Hence, I believe, the potential for crowding and shouldering is high at mealtimes, especially on days when the task of feeding falls to the family's teenage son, who has more interesting things on his mind than household chores. As a result, the dogs know all about waiting. In their yard, the afternoon wears on, and the sun creeps toward the Rockies. Feeding time comes, but nothing happens. Soon the sky is dark, but still no one comes. At last the neighborhood is quiet. Lights go on in the houses. The neighboring families gather in their kitchens. But in one yard, hunger and anxiety are mounting.

Did the uncertain atmosphere contribute to the custom? Could the dogs have sought to defuse the potentially flammable situation that arises when at last the kibbles rattle into the bowls? The five dogs don't recline at ease, as if to enhance enjoyment; rather, they lie stiffly, bowls between their forelegs, elbows flat, chests touching the ground, bellies slightly arched, knees up, and hocks down. They look like dogs down on command at obedience school. In this position they eat quickly and quietly, occasionally glancing at one another from the corners of their eyes. The custom makes for a controlled, orderly mealtime instead of a free-for-all in which the small but intelligent Rider could be steamrollered by the taller and heavier females.

Eventually, Rider's daughter, young Pearl, was sent to New England to join two older dogs in a household where pets were fed morning and evening. For a while, Pearl retained her unusual custom as best she could, standing up to eat the morning meal but dutifully lying down to eat the evening meal as she would have done back in Boulder. Even so, she soon gave up, and the strange custom never took root. If Pearl had been the alpha dog, it might have. But in her new home she wasn't even the alpha dog's daughter. Instead, her status was low, and the two old dogs didn't emulate her. So, after a few weeks, she chose to emulate them, and from then on stood up to eat both meals just as they did.

The dog who was observed weighing alternatives and making a decision was also a young female. Every day this dog took a walk with her owner and two other dogs, and every day they stopped at a river, where the young female invariably had a swim. On the day in question, however, something off the trail had drawn the young female away from the group, so that when the others stopped at the river, she wasn't with them. They turned to go home, as was their custom, and had gone about eighty feet down the trail when the young female, hot and ready for her daily bath, burst out of the bushes halfway between them and the river. Too late—they were leaving, and she had missed her swim. Poised beside the trail, she first looked to the right after her group, then looked to the left at the river, then looked to the right a second time, then looked once more at the water, made an instant decision, rushed full speed up the trail to the river, plunged in, quickly swam a few strokes, then turned back to the bank, leaped out, and tore after her group, not stopping to shake until she had caught up to them. (Virtually all dogs wait to shake themselves until they rejoin their group, especially if the others of the group did not swim; the need to shake seems secondary to the need to be close after having had a notably different experience from the others.)

The dog who was observed playing a game was a young male, a shepherd-Lab cross who had recently been given to an inactive, somewhat elderly couple who also owned an inactive, elderly female dog. The youngster had no one to play with—certainly not the older dog, who was very strict with him and tolerated no amusement of any kind. So the poor young dog often seemed at a loss, like a young person with no friends and nothing to do. One snowy night I saw him all by himself on a hillside near the house where he was staying, running fast with his nose to the ground. Whatever little rodent he was chasing seemed to be leading him in a big circle, which returned the rodent to the starting point, where the dog nuzzled for quite a while in one place—evidently at a hole where the quarry had gone to earth. But then, to my surprise, the dog started running again. Again with his nose to the ground, he made a second big circle that retraced the first. And again he nuzzled in one place, as if his quarry had again gone to earth.

I found all this very strange. What little creature would come up out of a safe hole right under a dog's nose in order to lead the dog around in a circle? And wouldn't the dog grab it when it came out? While I was puzzling over this, the dog rushed around the circle a third time, then a fourth, then a fifth and sixth. Each time his demeanor was the same—alert, excited, tail high and waving, nose to earth, as eager the last time as he had been the first. And when I went near for a look, I found, of course, that there was no quarry, and no hole either. The entire event had been a fantasy. This imaginative dog had been pretending.

The dog who adopted a human mannerism is my husband's dog, who amazed us all one hot day this past summer after my husband had bought himself an ice cream cone. As my husband took the first taste, he noticed that his dog was watching. So he offered the cone, expecting the dog to gobble it. But to everyone's astonishment, the dog politely licked a little ice cream just as my husband had done. My husband then licked a little more, and again offered it to the dog, who also licked a little more. In this way, taking turns, they ate the ice cream down to the cone. Then my husband took a bite. The dog watched him. Assuming that the dog would bolt the rest of the cone, my husband passed it on for what he thought would be the last time. But drawing back his lips to expose his little incisors, the dog took the most delicate of nibbles. Twice more my husband and the dog took turns biting the cone, until only the tip remained.

Astounding? Not really. For eight years, my husband and this dog have built a relationship of trust and mutual obligation, neither making unreasonable demands on the other or patronizing the other, or trying to subordinate the other, but each doing exactly what he wants, usually in the other's company. Only in such a setting, only when both participants consider themselves equals, could this scene have taken place. Only a dog who thought for himself, a dog who wasn't brainwashed by excessive training, a dog who depended on his own observations and imagination for guidance, would ever figure out the very human method of taking alternate bites as a form of sharing. After all, when two dogs share food, they eat simultaneously while respecting each other's feeding space, which is a little imaginary circle around the other's mouth. But the idea of taking alternate bites is totally human. Even so, the dog fathomed it, *and without ever having seen it done.* Who ate the tip of the cone? My husband ate it. The dog let him have the last turn.

Do dogs have thoughts and feelings? Of course they do. If they didn't, there wouldn't be any dogs. That being said, however, a book on dogs must by definition be somewhat anthropomorphic, and reasonably so, since our aversion to the label is misplaced. Using the experience of one's species to evaluate the experience of another species has been a useful tool to many of the great wildlife biologists. The more experienced the investigator, the more useful the tool. Consider George Schaller's observation of a mother leopard and her son: "At times [the two leopards] had ardent reunions, rubbing their cheeks and bodies sinuously and licking each other's face, obviously excited and delighted with the meeting. Witnessing such tenderness, I realized that these leopards merely masked their warm temperament and emotional depth beneath a cold exterior."[1]

In contrast is the observation of a former neighbor of mine, now deceased—a psychiatrist, actually—who saw a bird fly into the glass of his picture window and fall to earth, stunned. In a moment, a second bird swooped down, picked up the first, and flew away with it. In a quite moving anthropomorphization, the psychiatrist assumed that the second bird was a male, the mate of the first, and had come to her rescue. However, since birds never carry their loved ones, and grab other birds only to kill them, the second bird was surely not a helper at all but a predator taking advantage of the first bird's plight. If the psychiatrist had been more familiar with the ways of the natural world, he probably wouldn't have made that particular assumption.

We are not the only species to apply our values and our experience when interpreting other creatures. Dogs do it too, sometimes with no more luck than the psychiatrist. When a dog with a bone menaces a human observer, the dog actually assumes that the person wants the slimy, dirt-laden object,

[1] George Schaller, *Golden Shadows, Flying Hooves* (New York: Knopf, 1973, p. 196.

and is applying dog values, or cynomorphizing. Nevertheless, most animals, including dogs, constantly evaluate other species by means of empathetic observation. A dog of mine once assessed my mood, which was dark, over a distance of about one hundred yards, and changed his demeanor from cheery to bleak in response. He was in a pen that I was approaching, and as I rounded the corner he caught sight of me. I was sad at heart but not showing it in a way that any of the people around me had noticed, but the dog saw at once that something was wrong. Over the great distance he stared at me a moment, as if to be sure that he was really seeing what he thought he was seeing, and then, evidently deciding that his first impression had been accurate, he drooped visibly. I was so impressed with his acuity that I cheered up again, and so did he!

I was equally impressed by a female housecat, Lilac, whom I happened to be carrying home one evening, when on the way I decided to look in a nearby field to see if by chance any deer were grazing. I must have tensed a little as I got near the field, and perhaps walked a bit more quietly, but whatever it was, Lilac felt the change, instantly recognized it as a prelude to hunting, and leaned forward, ears up, eyes wide, claws sticking into my arm, ready to spring at whatever I might be stalking.

As a further note on anthropomorphism, the reader may notice references herein to a dog's smile. All dogs smile, which is to say their faces become pleasant and relaxed, with ears low, eyes half shut, lips soft and parted, and chin high. This is a dog smile. Yet a few dogs also emulate human smiles, and hence they themselves are anthropomorphizing. In the presence of human beings these dogs will draw back their lips grotesquely to bare their teeth, making the same face we make. At the same time, these dogs may also roll over to reveal their bellies submissively, showing that they understand exactly what our smiles mean.

And finally, anthropomorphism can help us interpret the act of showing the belly—the act that symbolizes what puppies do when submitting to adult dogs. By the act, dogs say to us, *Do as you will with us, since we are helpless puppies in your presence.* To understand the act, we can look at the human parallel: the way many religious people—Christians, for example—behave toward God. We call God the parent and ourselves his children. When we kneel to pray, we diminish our height, so that we look more like young children. Our prayerful position with raised eyes suggests that we are clasping God around the knees and looking up, as if he were facing us and looking straight down, not as if he were, say, off on the horizon. What's more, just as many of us pray at specified hours—upon getting up in the morning or going to bed at night, for instance—many dogs do their ritual submission at certain times of day. My husband's dog, for example, elects to show his belly to my husband right after they both get up in the morning. Why? No one knows for sure, but by now they both expect it.

Do dogs think we're God? Probably not. But just as we think of God's ways as mysterious, dogs find our ways capricious and mysterious, often with excellent reason. Every day the humane societies execute thousands of dogs who tried all their lives to do their very best by their owners. These dogs are killed not because they are bad but because they are inconvenient. So as we need God more than he needs us, dogs need us more than we need them, and they know it.

The Wolf Said to Francis

by A.G. Rochelle

Many stories are told about St. Francis of Assisi, the patron saint of animals. One legend states that when the town of Gubbio was plagued by a savage wolf who was killing sheep, Francis saved the town by persuading the wolf to change its ways. From that time on the wolf lived with the townspeople in peace and friendship. This poem imaginatively recreates the meeting between Francis and the wolf.

The wolf said to Francis
'You have more sense than some.
I will not spoil the legend;
Call me, and I shall come.

5 But in the matter of taming
Should you not look more near?
Those howlings come from humans.
Their hatred is their fear.

We are an orderly people.
10 Though great our pain and need,
We do not kill for torture.
We do not hoard for greed.

But the victim has the vision—
A gift of sorts that's given

15 As some might say, by history
And you, perhaps, by heaven.
Tomorrow or soon after
(Count centuries for days)
I see (and you may also
20 If you will turn your gaze)—

How the sons of man have taken
A hundredfold their share.
But the child of God, the creature,
Can rest his head nowhere.

25 See, sky and ocean empty,
The earth scorched to the bone;
By poison, gun, starvation
The last free creature gone.
But the swollen tide of humans
30 Sweeps on and on and on.

No tree, no bird, no grassland
Only increasing man,
And the prisoned beasts he feeds on —
Was *this* the heavenly plan?'

35 Francis stood there silent.
Francis bowed his head.
Clearly passed before him
All that the wolf had said.

Francis looked at his brother
40 He looked at the forest floor.
The vision pierced his thinking,
And with it, something more
That humans are stony listeners.

The legend stands as before.

The Man Who Was a Horse

by Julius Lester

Like Jack London, the cowboy in this story understands that to truly understand a wild creature, a human has to put himself in the creature's place.

It wasn't noon yet, but the sun had already made the Texas plains hotter than an oven. Bob Lemmons pulled his wide-brimmed hat tighter to his head and rode slowly away from the ranch

"Good luck, Bob!" someone yelled.

Bob didn't respond. His mind was already on the weeks ahead. He walked his horse slowly, being in no particular hurry. That was one thing he had learned early. One didn't capture a herd of mustang horses in a hurry. For all he knew, a mustang stallion might have been watching him at that very moment, and if he were galloping, the stallion might get suspicious and take the herd miles away.

Bob looked around him, and as far as he could see the land was flat, stretching unbroken like the cloudless sky over his head until the two seemed to meet. Nothing appeared to be moving except him on his horse, but he knew that a herd of mustangs could be galloping near the horizon line at that moment and he would be unable to see it until it came much closer.

He rode north that day, seeing no sign of mustangs until close to evening when he came across some tracks. He stopped and dismounted. For a long while he stared at the tracks until he was able to identify several of the horses. As far as he could determine, it seemed to be a small herd of a stallion, seven or eight mares, and a couple of colts. The tracks were no more than three days old and he half expected to come in sight of the herd the next day or two. A herd didn't travel in a straight line, but ranged back and forth within what the stallion considered his territory. Of course, that could be the size of a county. But Bob knew he was in it, though he had not seen a horse.

He untied his blanket from behind the saddle and laid it out on the ground. Then he removed the saddle from the horse and hobbled the animal to a stake. He didn't want a mustang stallion coming by during the night and stealing his horse. Stallions were good at that. Many times he had known them to see a herd of tame horses and, for who knew what reason, become attracted to one mare and cut her out of the herd.

He took his supper out of the saddlebags and ate slowly as the chilly night air seemed to rise from the very plains that a few short hours before had been too hot for a man to walk on. He threw the blanket around his shoulders, wishing he could make a fire. But if he had, the smell of woodsmoke in his clothes would have been detected by any herd he got close to.

After eating he laid his head back against his saddle and covered himself with his thick Mexican blanket. The chilliness of the night made the stars look to him like shining slivers of ice. Someone had once told him that the stars were balls of fire, like the sun, but Bob didn't feel them that way. But he wasn't educated, so he wouldn't dispute with anybody about it. Just because you gave something a name didn't mean that was what it actually was, though. The thing didn't know it had that name, so it just kept on being what it thought it was. And as far as he was concerned, people would be better off if they tried to know a thing like it knew itself. That was the only way he could ever explain to somebody how he was able to bring in a herd of wild horses by himself. The way other people did it was to go out in groups of two and three and run a herd until it almost dropped from exhaustion.

He guessed that was all right. It worked. But he couldn't do it that way. He knew he wouldn't want anybody running him to and fro for days on end, until he hardly knew up from down or left from right.

Even while he was still a slave, he'd felt that way about mustangs. Other horses too. But he had never known anything except horses. Born and raised on a ranch, he had legally been a slave until 1865, when the slaves in Texas were freed. He had been eighteen at the time and hadn't understood when Mr. Hunter had come and told him that he was free. That was another one of those words, Bob thought. Even as a child when his father told him he was a slave, he'd wondered what he meant. What did a slave look like? What did a slave feel like? He didn't think he had ever known. He and his parents had been the only colored people on the ranch and he guessed it wasn't until after he was "freed" that he saw another colored person. He knew sometimes, from the names he heard the cowboys use, that his color somehow made him different. He heard them talking about "fighting a war over the nigger," but it meant nothing to him. So when Mr. Hunter told him he was free, that he could go wherever he wanted to, he nodded and got on his horse and went on out to the range to see after the cattle like he was supposed to. He smiled to himself, wondering how Mr. Hunter had ever gotten the notion that he couldn't have gone where he wanted.

A few months after that he brought in his first herd of mustangs. He had been seeing the wild horses since he could remember. The first time had been at dusk one day. He had been playing near the corral when he happened to look toward the mesa and there, standing atop it, was a lone stallion. The wind blew against it and its mane and tail flowed in the breeze like tiny ribbons. The horse stood there for a long while; then, without warning, it suddenly wheeled and galloped away. Even now Bob remembered how seeing that horse had been like looking into a mirror. He'd never told anyone that, sensing that they would perhaps think him a little touched in the head. Many people thought it odd enough that he could bring in a herd of mustangs by himself. But, after that, whenever he saw one mustang or a herd, he felt like he was looking at himself.

One day several of the cowboys went out to capture a herd. The ranch was short of horses and no one ever thought of buying horses when there were so many wild ones. He had wanted to tell them that he would bring in the horses, but they would have laughed at him. Who'd ever heard of one man bringing in a herd? So he watched them ride out, saying nothing. A few days later they were back, tired and disgusted. They hadn't even been able to get close to a herd.

That evening Bob timidly suggested to Mr. Hunter that he be allowed to try. Everyone laughed. Bob reminded them that no one on the ranch could handle a horse like he could, that the horses came to him more than anyone else. The cowboys acknowledged that that was true, but it was impossible for one man to capture a herd. Bob said nothing else. Early the next morning he rode out alone, asking the cook to leave food in a saddlebag for him on the fence at the north pasture every day. Three weeks later the cowboys were sitting around the corral one evening and looked up to see a herd of mustangs galloping toward them, led by

Bob. Despite their amazement, they moved quickly to open the gate and Bob led the horses in.

That had been some twenty years ago, and long after Bob left the Hunter Ranch he found that everywhere he went he was known. He never had trouble getting a job, but capturing mustangs was only a small part of what he did. Basically he was just a cowboy who worked from sunrise to sunset, building fences, herding cattle, branding calves, pitching hay, and doing everything else that needed to be done.

Most cowboys had married and settled down by the time they reached his age, but Bob had long ago relinquished any such dream. Once he'd been in love with a Mexican girl, but her father didn't want her to marry a "nigger." Bob had been as confused as ever at being labeled that. He would never know what that word meant to old Jóse. But whatever it was, it was more than enough for him to stop Pilár from marrying Bob. After that he decided not to be in love again. It wasn't a decision he'd ever regretted. Almost every morning when he got up and looked at the sky lying full and open and blue, stretching toward forever, he knew he was married to something. He wanted to say the sky, but it was more than that. He wanted to say everything, but he felt that it was more than that too. How could there be more than everything? He didn't know, but there was.

The sun awakened him even before the first arc of its roundness showed over the horizon. He saddled his horse and rode off, following the tracks he had discovered the previous evening. He followed them west until he was certain they were leading him to the Pecos River. He smiled. Unless it was a herd traveling through, they would come to that river to drink every day. Mustangs never went too far from water, though they could go for days without a drop if necessary.

The Pecos was still some distance ahead, but he felt his horse's body quiver slightly, and she began to strain forward against his tight hold on the reins. She smelled the water.

"Sorry honey. But that water's not for you," he told the horse. He wheeled around and galloped back in the direction of the ranch until he came to the outermost edge of what was called the west pasture. It was still some miles from the ranch house itself, and today Bob couldn't see any cattle grazing up there.

But on the fence rail enclosing the pasture was a saddlebag filled with food. Each day one of the cowboys would bring a saddlebag of food up there and leave it for him. He transferred the food to his own saddlebags. He was hungry but would wait until evening to eat. The food had to have time to lose its human odor, an odor that mustangs could pick out of the slightest breeze. He himself would not venture too close to the horses for another few days, not until he was certain that his own odor had become that of his horse.

He rode southward from the pasture to the banks of the Nueces River. There he dismounted, took the saddle off his horse, and let her drink her fill and wade in the stream for a while. It would be a few days before she could drink from the Pecos. The mustangs would have noticed the strange odor of horse and man together, and any good stallion would have led his mares and colts away. The success of catching mustangs, as far as Bob was concerned, was never to hurry. If necessary he would spend two weeks getting a herd accustomed to his distant presence once he was in sight of them.

He washed the dust from his face and filled his canteen. He lay down under a tree, but its shade didn't offer much relief from the heat of high noon. The day felt like it was on fire and Bob decided to stay where he was until the sun began its downward journey. He thought Texas was probably the hottest place in the world. He didn't know, not having traveled much. He had been to Oklahoma, Kansas, New Mexico, Arizona, and Wyoming on cattle drives. Of all the places, he liked Wyoming the most, because of the high mountains. He'd never seen anything so high. There were mountains in Texas, but nothing like that. Those mountains just went up and up and up until it seemed they would never stop. But they always did, with snow on the top. After a few days though he wasn't sure that he did like the mountains. Even now he wasn't sure. The mountains made him feel that he was penned in a corral, and he was used to spaces no smaller than the sky. Yet he remembered Wyoming with fondness and hoped that some year another cattle drive would take him there.

The heat had not abated much when Bob decided to go north again and pick up his trail. He would camp close to the spot where his mare had first smelled the Pecos. That was close enough for now. In the days following, Bob moved closer to the river until one evening he saw the herd come streaming out of the hills, across the plain, and to the river. He was some distance away, but he could see the stallion lift his head and sniff the breeze. Bob waited. Although he couldn't know for sure, he could feel the stallion looking at him, and for a tense moment Bob didn't know if the horse would turn and lead the herd away. But the stallion lowered his head and began to drink and the other horses came down to the river. Bob sighed. He had been accepted.

The following day he crossed the river and picked up the herd's trail. It was not long after sunrise before he saw them grazing. He went no closer, wanting only to keep them in sight and, most important, make them feel his presence. He was glad to see that after a moment's hesitation the stallion went back to grazing.

Bob felt sorry for the male horse. It always had to be on guard against dangers. If it relaxed for one minute, that just might be the minute a nearby panther would choose to strike, or another stallion would challenge him for the lead of the herd, or some cowboys would throw out their ropes. He wondered why a stallion wanted the responsibility. Even while the horses were grazing, Bob noticed that the stallion was separate, over to one side, keeping a constant lookout. He would tear a few mouthfuls of grass from the earth, then raise his head high, looking and smelling for danger.

At various times throughout the day Bob moved a few hundred yards closer. He could see it clearly now. The stallion was brown, the color of the earth. The mares and colts were black and brown. No sorrels or duns in this herd. They were a little smaller than his horse. But all mustangs were. Their size, though, had nothing to do with their strength or endurance. There was no doubt that they were the best horses. He, however, had never taken one from the many herds he had brought in. It wasn't that he wouldn't have liked one. He would have, but for him to have actually ridden one would have been like taking a piece of the sky and making a blanket. To ride with them when they were wild was all right. But he didn't think any man was really worthy of riding one, even though he brought them in for that purpose.

By the sixth day he had gotten close enough to the herd that his presence didn't attract notice. The following day he moved closer until he and his mare were in the herd itself. He galloped with the herd that day, across the plain, down to the river, up into the hills. He observed the stallion closely, noting that it was a good one. The best stallions led the herd from the rear. A mare always led from the front. But it was only at the rear that a stallion could guard the herd and keep a mare from running away. The stallion ran up and down alongside the herd, biting a slow mare on the rump or ramming another who threatened to run away or to bump a third. The stallion was king, Bob thought, but he worked. It didn't look like much fun.

He continued to run with the herd a few days more. Then came the crucial moment when, slowly, he would begin to give directions of his own, to challenge the stallion in little ways until he had completely taken command of the herd and driven the stallion off. At first he would simply lead the herd in the direction away from the one the stallion wanted to go, and just before the stallion became enraged, he would put it back on course. He did this many times, getting the stallion confused as to whether or not there was a challenger in his midst. But enough days of it and the stallion gradually wore down, knowing that something was happening, but unable to understand what. When Bob was sure the herd was in his command, he merely drove the stallion away.

Now came the fun. For two weeks Bob led the herd. Unlike the stallion, he chose to lead from the front, liking the sound and feel of the wild horses so close behind. He led them to the river and watched happily as they splashed and rolled in the water. Like the stallion, however, he kept his eyes and ears alert for any sign of danger. Sometimes he would pretend he heard something when he hadn't and would lead the herd quickly away simply as a test of their responsiveness to him.

At night he stopped, unsaddled his horse, and laid

out his blanket. The herd grazed around him. During all this time he never spoke a word to the horses, not knowing what effect the sound of a voice might have on them. Sometimes he wondered what his own voice sounded like and even wondered if after some period of inactivity, he would return to the ranch and find himself able only to snort and neigh, as these were the only sounds he heard. There were other sounds though, sounds that he couldn't reproduce, like the flaring nostrils of the horses when they were galloping, the dark, bulging eyes, the flesh quivering and shaking. He knew that he couldn't hear any of these things—not with his ears at least. But somewhere in his body he heard every ripple of muscles and bending of bones.

The longer he was with the herd, the less he thought. His mind slowly emptied itself of anything relating to his other life and refilled with sky, plain, grass, water, and shrubs. At these times he was more aware of the full-bodied animal beneath him. His own body seemed to take on a new life and he was aware of the wind against his chest, of the taut muscles in his strong legs and the strength of his muscles in his arms, which felt to him like the forelegs of his horses. The only thing he didn't feel he had was a tail to float in the wind behind him.

Finally, when he knew that the herd would follow him anywhere, it was time to take it in. It was a day he tried to keep away as long as possible. But even he began to tire of going back to the west pasture for food and sometimes having to chase a horse that had tried to run away from the herd. He had also begun to weary of sleeping under a blanket on the ground every night. So one day, almost a month after he had left, he rode back toward the ranch until he saw one of the cowhands and told him to get the corral ready.

Tomorrow he was bringing them in.

The following morning he led the herd on what he imagined was the ride of their lives. Mustangs were made to run. All of his most vivid memories were of mustangs, and he remembered the day he had seen a herd of what must have been at least a thousand of them galloping across the plains. The earth was a dark ripple of movement, like the swollen Nueces at floodtime. And though his herd was much smaller, they ran no less beautifully that day.

Then toward evening, Bob led them east, galloping, galloping, across the plains. And as he led them toward the corral, he knew that no one could ever know these horses by riding on them. One had to ride with them, feeling their hooves pound and shake the earth, their bodies glistening so close by that you could see the thin straight hairs of their shining coats. He led them past the west pasture, down the slope, and just before the corral gate, he swerved to one side, letting the horses thunder inside. The cowboys leaped and shouted, but Bob didn't stay to hear their congratulations. He slowed his mare to a trot and then to a walk to cool her off. It was after dark when he returned to the ranch.

He took his horse to the stable, brushed her down, and put her in a stall for a well-earned meal of hay. Then he walked over to the corral, where the mustangs milled restlessly. He sat on the rail for a long while, looking at them. They were only horses now. Just as he was only a man.

After a while he climbed down from the fence and went into the bunkhouse to go to sleep.

Unsentimental Mother

by Sally Carrighar

The call of the wild brought a mature Buck back to his ancestral roots. How might it feel to begin life in the wild? Sally Carrighar spent about ten years in the arctic studying Eskimos and arctic wildlife. In "Unsentimental Mother" she offers this account of the first few weeks in the life of an Arctic seal.

In the last weeks before the young hair seal was born, his mother was much alone. When she swam about under the ice pack, she stayed away from the channels below the recently frozen leads. In those lighter lanes, with thin, translucent ice above, the males would go sweeping by, several of them together. The female, with trancelike interest, was exploring beneath the thicker ice which had been frozen all winter. She was hunting for chinks in which she could make some new exit-holes. She had her own holes, several for breathing and one large enough so that she could crawl out on the top of the ice, but they were too far apart for a cub with small lungs. He would need to rise frequently for a breath, and to rest on the surface.

When the seal found a place that seemed right, she began work by breathing upon the under side of the ice. As it softened, she nibbled and clawed it out, forming a vertical tunnel. Her hind flippers held her wherever she needed to be, the webs rippling and curling, propelling her up or down. She must often stop and swim to one of her own holes for air, but finally she had completed a chimney; then two others, close together, all opening up through the ice and wide, so that a cub could climb out of the water. They froze over again each day, but the seal would bunt out the new ice with her nose and break off the pieces around the edge with her foreflippers. She kept the holes ready.

A larger task was the shelter, the "seal's igloo," the Eskimos named it, where the cub would be born and spend his first days. It was to be on the top of the ice but under a snowdrift, with its only door down to the ocean below. When she was through the ice, up within the drift, the seal scooped out her den, leaving an unbroken roof of snow. The entrancehole was surrounded by a floor wide enough to provide a resting place for a mother and cub.

After the shelter was finished, the female seemed even more shy, more withdrawn, as she lay apart on the ice or swam through the water below it. Fewer and fewer things could attract her interest. Her emotions appeared to be like the den—cleared to receive the cub.

She had a difficult time bearing him, for his weight was nearly a fifth of hers. Her groans filled the little house. But finally, wrapped in a transparent membrane, he lay on the floor. She split open the tissue to let him breathe, and tore it off, and licked her small cub all over. His coat was wet, and she dried it by rubbing it with her foreflipper, which had its five fingers connected with webs of furred skin. The little seal's coat was not in any way like his mother's. Hers was dark-spotted gray, its hairs thin and nearly straight, while his was a long, very dense, crinkly white fuzz.

The night he was born was starry and still, and the cold over the Northern sea was as biting as acid. The cub was not nuzzling his mother for milk—not yet. He was shivering, and his cry was a heart-melting whimper. His mother lay close against him and continued to stroke his fur.

Suddenly the caress of her flippers stopped. Her breathing, all but her heartbeat, stopped. She was hearing the squeak of sled-runners on snow, and a fluttering whistle, an Eskimo imitating a ptarmigan's voice to keep his dogs sharp. The squeaks and the whistling ceased, and the snow creaked under footsteps. The seal wrapped her flipper around the cub, catching her claws in his wool, and slid nearer the exit-hole. A harpoon drove down into the den, and the sweep of an arm broke the roof. But the mother had dived with her young one.

She dared not come up in one of the new holes near the igloo. Could the cub survive the long swim to her old exit-hole? As fast as she could with her burden and her new weakness, she sped through the water beneath the ice. She knew the route well: past the rounded corners of the submerged ice caves, under a late-frozen lead, then a straight stretch below a smooth ceiling of ice. Only a little farther— but the cub was squirming convulsively, badly needing a breath. His mother could see her hole up ahead. When she reached it and lifted the cub's nose into the air he gasped and relaxed.

Even here she did not come out; she could not risk being found. She took the small seal below to the floor of the ocean, where she lay and waited, holding him with her flipper. Frequently she would rise to let him breathe. He should be out on the top of the ice having his first meal of milk, but the hunter was still too near. Apparently he would stay all night. The ice over this east end of Norton Sound was frozen into one vast, unbroken field. The Eskimos drove their dog sleds out to the edge, to the open water, for the better chance there to find seals. Coming so far, twenty-five miles or more, they could not go back to land in one day conveniently. When they were tired, they searched for a seal's igloo in which to lie down on the reindeer skins they had brought.

On this night the seal mother cautiously reared her head several times to look over the width of the ice. The man had vanished into her partly demolished den, but the dogs were outside. Each time she came to the surface, one or more of the dogs would rise, sniffing in her direction. They were getting her scent, but they did not bark and arouse the hunter.

The cub was becoming more limp. Now his body hung slackly away from her flipper, and yet she could only wait, she could not put him up into the air and excite the dogs. Slowly the sky became pale over the distant mountains behind the shore. The sun widened above a summit. Its shine on the snow crept closer across the ice pack, throwing shadows out from each little knob and great hummock and gradually pulling the shadows back.

The next time the mother lifted her head, the man was untying the dogs from their stakes in the ice. He stepped on the runners and started the dogs, for a time guiding them in a prowling course near the igloo, doubtless hoping to find its owner. Then he turned away west, toward the water just visible on the horizon. The dogs became smaller, only the upright shape of the man could be seen, and he too disappeared behind one of the hummocks of ice cakes. The mother seal pushed her cub, unconscious now, onto the surface.

The snap in the air and the brightness revived him.

For the first time alert, he started to live. But living was only a lack, a desperate want, a fumbling for—what? There it was—silky smooth cream, rich and warm, going down his throat. Pull it harder! He needed so much and probably never would get enough. The milk was filling his mouth faster than he could swallow, and yet hunger, a fearful blind dread, was not stilled. Milk was a thing that must be, and it might not be. It could stop. The seal's flippers, like small hands, curled inward, involuntarily trying to grasp, to hold.

When his stomach was full, the cub still sensed a need. He pushed forward against his mother, and cried. The sheltering body came nearer, until he was almost enclosed by it, covered and safe. A caressing tongue stroked his nose, up over his forehead, around his ears. He pushed his head closer to make the stroking more firm. His mother was rubbing his fur with her flipper, too; she was doing her wild, instinctive best to make him feel loved and soothed, and finally the cub fell asleep.

All through the day she did not leave him. If he was awake and she had stopped stroking or licking his wool he would nudge her, an eloquent asking. He did not open his eyes more than to glimpse the gray fur at his side.

On the seal's second day, when curiosity moved him to look around, he found that a pressure ridge of ice cakes towered over him. They were piled up in mammoth disorder, with jagged ice pinnacles spiking the top. The ridge, called an *eewoonuck* by the Eskimos, rose from the floor of the ice field abruptly, as mountains are sometimes thrust up from plains. But the slopes and crevices in the *eewoonuck* were not arranged as they are on a mountain, which shows the stresses that built it up and the carving of valleys by water. The ice mountain was wreckage.

The seal lay in a snow meadow close to its base. Farther away other *eewoonucks* broke the expanse, with flat snow fields around them. No sand was here, no sunken logs with root-crowns mazy and interesting, no swaying seaweed with small darting fish and lazy large ones exploring among the fronds, no shellfish speeding about by clapping their shells together. Those, in the depths below, he would learn about later. On the ice, here, no life was found; therefore no death—as if the world were just being formed, all new as yet and unspoiled, no dust, no death, only the lovely light and the clean sparkling crystal, suitable for a small, new creature, himself so white. But this realm of purity was wide, silent, and motionless. *Where was his mother?* The cub's cry was a shriek.

She was near. She splashed up at once and stretched out beside him. His sudden loneliness had been a slight shock, and so now as he nursed, the end of each breath would catch in his throat. As always, his mother was stroking his fur. Was his woolly first coat beginning to shed? By the time that his second, thinner coat had replaced it, the cub would have built up an insulating layer of fat. He then would have had all of her milk that he needed, and if she had taught him and cared for him well, she could go on to other urgent concerns. She drew her claws through his fuzz. It was tight, but it soon would loosen.

He slept, but not for long. His short period of dependence could not be leisurely. He awoke with his mother's flipper encircling him; next he was down in the water. She swam just below him, to give him a chance to cling to her back. As he felt the thrust of her muscles, the young seal had an impulse to push the same way. Safe with her support, he too curved his spine right and left and clapped the webs of his hind feet, helping to drive ahead. He was enjoying this exercise when without warning he was alone. He thrashed about, no longer able to get any grip on the water, which seemed all looseness now, broken softness. And he needed air! At the surge of his panic, his mother's strong body rose under his and they shot to the surface. But immediately he was dragged under again, and kept there until he could take a few strokes without help. Then she allowed him to go above. He caught into the edge of his exit-hole with his claws and hoisted himself—now he was back on top. He looked around anxiously. Yes, she was coming out too. He still wanted to feel protected, although he had had his first inkling of self-reliance, he had learned that a seal can swim.

She taught him to forage. As long as he kept his coat of thick fuzz he could not swim fast enough to catch fish easily, but she took him down into the water so often that soon he could find his way among the dark, glossy caverns at the submerged bases of the great *eewoonucks*. He was not startled now when flounders flapped up from the floor of the sea, like patches of mud which had drifted loose and were being wafted away. He saw king crabs fighting with slow, deadly persistence, and jellyfish throwing the living webs of their tentacles over young trout. Once a fish larger than he, a whiting, turned into an ice cave with indolent power and disappeared. But the schools of tomcod were most interesting. Spaced out evenly, they would weave through the water, feeding themselves by keeping their open mouths moving ahead. They swam at a dreamy pace, all together making their softly smooth, unhurried turns. The cub's mother flashed forward and took a tomcod in her mouth, and then worked it around until its head faced toward her throat so its fins and scales would go down comfortably. The cub did not want to eat a tomcod yet, but he did snap up a shrimp and found he could chew it.

On the top of the ice, his mother would move away over the snow while he followed. He learned how to arch his spine as she did, holding hind flippers and tail off the surface, and hitching himself along with his foreflippers, which reached ahead and gave a big push, bouncing him forward upon his belly. Always his mother would bring him back to the water-hole. He must stay near it most of the time, facing it so that one thrust with his flippers would send him below. For at this season his only enemies would approach over the ice. And finally his mother played with him. She would take the fur of his neck in her teeth and teasingly shake him. In the same spirit he snapped. She nuzzled his belly, and he rolled on his back and struck at her. She tumbled him, always so quick that when his teeth sought her skin she was out of reach. At the end she would let him catch one of her flippers. He sucked on it tensely. Perhaps with so strong a pull he could hold her forever.

All young hair seals demand their mothers' attention more than most land animals do, perhaps because they receive care for so short a time. In the seas around Norton Sound, the cubs' new gray swimming coats are grown out in two or three weeks. By that time the cubs have put on a layer of blubber that triples their weight. Needing so much milk so quickly, they plead for it almost without pause, and to make sure that they get it, nature seems to promote great affection between a seal mother and cub. The young soon learn how to make themselves very appealing, and for as long as they stay the mother seals are demonstrative. This bond was even more close in the case of the cub who was snatched from his igloo almost before he had started to breathe. His mother had had to spend more than the usual amount of time with him, for she did not have any place where she could hide him with safety, and he had become a bit spoiled. His forehead was constantly puckered, as if some uneasiness shadowed him, and when he was alone, his eyes would become huge and round, and he would stretch his head high, trying to find his guardian. Within a few days he could sit up, balancing on one hip, with a foreflipper braced on the snow, while he turned his head far around so that he had a view of the whole horizon. If his mother was not in sight, he would begin a shrieking—desperate-sounding, and nearly always she came immediately.

But one afternoon when he called, she heaved herself out of the hole in the ice—and then wandered away. Crying, he followed. She was not playing, he sensed; she was trying to leave him. She stopped, but when he came close, she did not give him her milk at once. She kept looking off between two of the *eewoonucks*. He nudged her several times, and then finally she did turn sidewise. But why had she almost refused him?

She stirred. And the cub stopped nursing. For he could scent something new in the air. He sat up. Over his mother's side he saw, at the exit-hole, the head of another seal. It was a large head, gray like his mother's, with immense dark eyes somewhat bolder than hers. The cub's mother lifted her nose to grasp the new odor. The head of the stranger sank out of sight, rose again, and then started an up-and-down ducking. The seal mother turned her head over her back to watch, and the male's rhythmical motions continued.

A new alarm creased the cub's forehead, not fear of the male exactly, for the cub had no impulse to flee. And yet something was very wrong. He moved closer against his mother, and when she did not respond, pushed into her fur. Still he could not distract her. She swung her head forward, no longer seeming to notice the male, but she did not show the cub any affection. She brushed her cheek with her foreflipper, and sighed, a deep, collapsing breath. Finally she began to smooth the cub's fur, behind his ears and along his chin. He felt only a little happier. He closed his eyes for a sleep but, opening them again, he saw that his mother's claws were full of white infantile wool.

In only another day or two the new situation was set: for every moment of her attention, the cub must compete with the male. His wailing rang over the ice incessantly. Sometimes, to be near her, the cub would go down in the water. She seemed to feel more responsible for him there and would keep close to him as he swam about. The male was the one who was doing the handsome swimming. Marvelous were the swift boiling somersaults, the swirling in which the big seal seemed as limber as water itself, and the speed with which he would rush past the mother and cub. That exhibition of strength would swing currents around them. In the dark water the eyeshine of the two adult seals would flash. And then, while she was watching the male, the mother might suddenly turn and play with the cub. The big seal would have to compete with *him*. It was so on the top of the ice too. The cub's mother ignored him at times, but at other times, although the male would be there and doing his best to be entertaining, she would nuzzle the little seal, play with him in the most absorbed way. It would seem then as if nothing the large seal could do would distract her. But she heard none of the cub's cries when she and the male were playing. For they did play, a grand big frolic, slapping and nudging each other and tumbling in and out of the exit-hole. It was more splendid than anything the small seal could do.

Keeping pace with the new events was the change in the cub's coat. It was now a patchwork of yellow-gray fur and tufts of an infant's white wool. The wool still impeded his swimming, while the fur made him conspicuous on the snow, so that he did not seem to belong anywhere for the present, neither down in the water nor up on the ice. A day came when his mother would never respond except when hunger put its particular tone in the cub's voice—although, at noon, she rose from the water when he had not called, and fed him, and afterwards lay on the ice beside him. She had brought up a string of seaweed, caught in her flipper. The cub sniffed it and snapped at it, pulling it off—a make-believe rival. He was having such a fine bout with it that he did not even notice his mother's leaving when she slipped down the hole.

She never came back. After his play with the seaweed he fell asleep and woke only hungry enough to whimper. But by nightfall he was quite empty, and when the sun dropped behind the *eewoonuck*, and its shadow stretched out to enclose the cub, he began to feel frightened. He sat up, turning his head to search over the silent and lifeless snow. Soon all the sunlight was gone. The stars were like frost on the sky, a sheet of sparkles that dropped its chill over the cub, while the ice breathed its cold up around him.

Perhaps his mother was over behind the

eewoonuck. Once she and the male had gone there in their frolicking. The cub hobbled along her trail to the ridge of the ice cakes, around its end, and found the place where his mother's trail joined with the male's. But she was not there, and the ice pack seemed even emptier on this side. The cub hurried back to the water-hole. She could be there now! As eagerly as if he had heard her splash, he pulled himself forward. When he could see the hole, and no mother beside it, he still hurried. Such a need as his surely must find its answer.

All through the night the little seal cried. He demanded, he begged that his mother come. If he had not been depending on her so much, he might have found food for himself; he might have gone down in the water-hole, and that would have been more practical, for hour by hour the cold was closing the hole with ice. In the morning, when the cub dropped his nose toward the hole, it was solid. He might have broken it even then if he tried. Instead he stayed in the air where he could make his cries heard, and by night the ice had become thick and firm. He had lost his chance to reach all the nourishing creatures down in the seas and he had lost his escape.

Three days and nights passed. Except when he wore himself out and must sleep, he called with never a stop, so regularly that one could believe a young seal breathed like this, with a shriek every time he emptied his lungs of air. Finally he started out on a new search over the ice. Before he had gone beyond many *eewoonucks,* he heard a sound which could have been his own echo, unceasing and shrill. He went toward it, and in rounding the end of a pressure ridge found another small seal. When the other caught sight of him, he sat up and with large and astonished eyes watched him advance. The stranger had lost all of his crinkly wool; he was as smooth and sleek as an adult seal. But he too had a cub's fright and loneliness. The two sniffed each other. While they were getting acquainted at last there was silence.

The seal started back to his ice-locked hole. Would the other come? Yes, he followed. As often happens when animals move from one place to another, one proved that he was the leader. The seal retraced his trail, but when they had reached the frozen hole, no mother was there; they had nothing to do but start calling again. Now the duet of cries was impelled less by loneliness than by hunger. Neither cub had had food for several days. They were prepared for this lean time when they would begin their own foraging; because of the excess of milk they had had, they still were more fat than any young creature, even in arctic cold, needed to be. But they were very uncomfortable. Sometimes their misery would not let them rest, and they wandered about. At the foot of the ridge of ice cakes they found a hollow, enclosed by the big broken blocks. They spent more and more time there, always sleeping within its shelter.

Thus far in his life the seal had heard only the voices and splashing of his own kind, and the cracking of ice—nothing else, no sound under the whole immense sky. Even the wind had been still. But a night came when strands of clouds were drawing across the moon, and the air started to prowl. It was not yet blowing in any one direction. Swirling this way and that, faster when it spun into a nook or cranny, it seemed like a predator, whipping among the ice blocks with a low stinging hiss and turning away, an impatient and searching breath.

By morning the wind was steady. It was blowing from off the land, over the ice to the open sea. The snow previously fallen was lifted, more of it as the wind gained force, until soon the driving, blinding white mist hid everything farther away than the seal's own length. The orphans were snug in their cave, but the snow sifted in at the entrance. And the sound of the wind was a roaring confusion, a slapping and beating close to the ice, and a whistling above, as the wind went streaming over sharp slices of ice on the top of the ridge. It was a tearing, mangling wind.

Each moment felt like the storm's climax: this now was the hardest a wind could blow, this attack was its strongest. Or so it seemed; yet for two days its speed and its power increased. All sensations were one—the thundering wind, the cold, the near-darkness, and snow, all combined in a tumult. The small seal was numb with exhaustion. He could only cling to his life, holding onto the warmth in his veins, the breath in his lungs, by a firmness that did not need to be conscious. Just hold.

The first warning of a new danger was slight—a quivering of the ice under his belly. Almost at once it was more, a crunching, a grinding, felt wherever he turned, as if some animal's teeth were gnawing the seal's own bones. He sat up, his eyes wide and alarmed. His companion also had roused. The seal hunched himself to the cave entrance. The only thing he found changed was the shine on the ice. Now the surface was gleaming and slick, all the snow blown away in the sea or shaped into fins of drift off the pressure ridges. The wind had beaten the drifts until they were glazed. Everything in the seal's view appeared brittle-hard—and the sickening vibration continued.

The wind caught the breath out of his lungs. He gasped and turned back. The orphan had moved, trying to fit himself deeper into his corner. The seal lay down near him . . . but could not rest. He hobbled again to the entrance, and barked. He wanted the other to follow, but the small stranger did not respond, except that he opened his eyes and closed them again. He had flattened himself up against an ice block and seemed to be comforted by its solid touch. The seal too would have welcomed that reassurance, but somehow the cave was a place where one should not be. A stronger impulse was checking the seal's wish to hide.

He ventured away from the *eewoonuck,* out onto the icy, wide, sheerly unprotected expanse. The sun was setting. Breaking through layers of cloud, it was streaking the sky with brilliance, and streaking the ice below—where the slashes of light widely shifted. Swinging too was the ridge's shadow. For the pack was in motion. It had broken away from its anchorage on the shore and a flood tide had raised the ice where it was grounded along a sandbar. Floating free then, it had been propelled west by the wind's offshore pressure. The whole field of it, twenty-five miles wide, was being blown out of Norton Sound to the Bering Sea, where the large pack of arctic ice was consolidated. As the wind pushed the shore-ice along, driving upon its variously placed ridges, the vast field broke into many ice islands. Screwed by the wind and tide, these were swirling and grinding together, crashing and heaving. The seal was stunned by the colliding of tons of ice, buckling upward and falling back with a scream of slipped surfaces and a roar as of mountains crumpling.

The seal suddenly felt the same panic that swept him when he had first tried to swim and he and the water went flaccid. He could no longer stay out here, alone and exposed to the violence! Hurrying back to the cave, he found the other seal in his crevice, trembling. The two curled up together, a tight huddle, sharing their warmth and their fright. But the seal could not rest. To be in the shelter was comforting—yet was not right. He went out again, moving along the foot of the ridge, and at the end, saw that the ice on the other side of the *eewoonuck* had split off from this part of the field. The open sea lay ahead. The seal's ridge, his area of the shore-ice, was now the prow of the whole wind-driven mass.

The moon, piercing through tattered clouds, showed how fast the ice was advancing into the waves. The seal went to the edge, yearning to be in the water. He dropped his nose over the brink. But the steep parapet overtook bits of seaweed and driftwood so fast that a small seal would surely be swept underneath, and suffocate there unless he happened to find a breathing-hole where the ice was not grinding.

He drew back, not to return to the nook, but to go out again on the level expanse, on the glare ice where nothing hid any part of the sky with its clouds gashed by moonlight, and nothing interrupted the sweep of the wind. To hide in the only way that he could, the seal drew his head far back into his coat with its lining of blubber. He watched his cave entrance for some sign that the other would leave the shelter and join him here on the wasteland of ice. But the shadow between the blocks showed no blur of movement. The seal's own instinct had prompted him to forsake consolation. All over the ice that night young seals were facing the same hard choice. More than half left the ridges, but some did not heed, or perhaps did not hear, the intuitive warning. Like the seal's companion, they stayed in the hideaways they had found.

They were speeding into the black water-smoke of

the Bering Sea. It was mid-morning when the seal on his racing ice saw through the black screen the edge of the Bering Sea ice pack. Spray from the open water had frozen upon its rim, which now had the look of a long wave, perpetually breaking. Pressure ridges lifted their shining heights from the pack, but not at the side where the Norton Sound ice was approaching. Toward that low surface the ice on which the seal rode was advancing with three days' momentum behind it.

The seal watched the foamy brink of the Bering Sea pack loom larger and clearer. It was so close now that back upon it a short way he could see a curious animal. For an instant it seemed to be an ice hummock with snow-rounded outlines, but it moved—a polar bear, lifting his head, sniffing into the wind. No doubt he was catching the scent of the seal, who raised his own head to see over the strip of black water, which was narrowing, shrinking. It was gone—

The crash knocked the seal nearly unconscious, but through his daze he could watch the frozen wave on the Bering Sea pack ride right up his pressure ridge, off its top, a great slice of ice that pushed on until it became a wide cornice that cracked off from its own weight and collapsed down the nearer slope. At the end of his old ridge a gigantic new *eewoonuck* formed, as the floors of the ice fields struck and, buckling up to a vastly high summit, tumbled back on both sides.

Debris from the mighty impact came smashing and screeching over the ice far enough for the blocks to have struck the seal, but they did not. They stopped; the splitting and cracking spread out to remote areas of both packs. Finally the echoes of the collision had ceased. A strange animal somewhere was bellowing with pain, but otherwise all was silent. The great slabs that had crossed the seal's ridge had demolished his shelter in falling. Where the cave had been, covered now with a block of transparent ice, lay his companion, quiet and only a little too flattened to seem alive.

The tumult went out of the seal's senses. He sat up to look around—and a movement on top of the new *eewoonuck* caught his eye. It was the polar bear, whose immense body was clambering over the ice boulders. The bear paused and stretched out his head. His nose, far in advance of his shoulders, was weaving snake-wise as, with his poor sight, the bear tried to catch the exact direction of the seal's scent. It apparently came to him clearly, for now he was hastening down the crevices of the ridge.

Where to go! Quickly the seal must hide! Looking about, frantic, he found that near him were veins of slush, wholly demolished ice. Could he get through to the water?

He dived into the slush but did not sink. He pushed with his nose and his shoulders, squirming and driving himself below with his foreflippers. Now he stood on his head, boring down and down. A claw grazed his hind flipper, but the bear must not have realized what he touched. If the great paw scooped again into the slush, the seal did not feel it, and the vein of soft ice was not wide enough to admit the huge bulk of the bear.

After pushing down twice his own length, the seal was below the pack. He swam along under it, hardly knowing what he was seeking. But there in front of him was a great chaotic break in the ice, admitting more light—a tunnel under the pressure ridge that extended up into the air, safe, a haven.

In the long dim cavern, roofed with ice blocks, the

seal climbed up onto a ledge. A black and white sea pigeon stood with its scarlet feet awash, eating a small fish, a blenny. The sight of the bird enjoying its meal reminded the seal of his hunger. He dived, straight into a school of tomcod, and caught one of them. Back in the cavern he shifted the tomcod around in his mouth and swallowed it, relishing this first taste of fish. He dived again and after a short, sharp chase captured another. The chase as well as the flavor seemed good.

Nature, the unsentimental mother, had challenged the young wistful seal. Thrown into danger he had successfully met the test, and because he had solved his own difficulties he had matured. He was no longer hungry or frightened, and he was no longer lonely, for he was not searching now for anyone who was gone.

Through a chink in the *eewoonuck* over his head, an animal's breath steamed down. It carried a scent that was new to the seal—that of an arctic fox. The fox could not reach the seal here where he lay with his foreflipper curled into water, and in any case water was safety under the ice. Water was home.

Long Duel

by Robert Murphy

The feelings of love, loyalty, and responsibility Buck had for John Thornton did not die when the man was killed. To what lengths might a person or animal go to avenge the death of a hero?

It was the dog that brought Yancy back into Jake Fischer's mind again after so many years: Yancy the debonair, the intrepid, cool hunter who had once stood up to a bear with nothing but a knife to prove to himself that he wasn't afraid of fear, the man Jake had so tremendously admired. For Jake had been victimized by an overactive imagination in those youthful days, and afraid of many things; it was natural that Yancy had become a hero to him, that he had struggled desperately to impose Yancy's code upon himself.

This had been one of the things that formed him; it had never gone out of his life; but the quiet uneventfulness of the intervening years had pushed it back into his subconscious. He surely wasn't thinking about it as he rode home from jury duty in Mountain City, but every step the horse took brought Yancy and a boyhood fear closer to him again.

Jake had no intimation of this as he rode along the twisting, rocky trail with his collar turned up against the afternoon chill in the mountain air. He wasn't paying much attention to the horse, which had been bred in the Great Smokies and knew its way well enough. His strong, stocky body functioned with unconscious and sympathetic skill to ease the horse, and his broad, darkly pleasant face, with its tanned cheeks and candid brown eyes, was preoccupied. He was thinking of what the lawyer from Elizabethton had said when court was over, the lawyer's talk about wild boars.

Somebody in North Carolina had imported a couple of them from the Harz Mountains back in 1912, the lawyer said, which had interbred with wild hogs; the progeny of these matings had crossed the mountains into Tennessee. They were as fierce and strong as any animal in the world, the lawyer said, mean as the devil and quick as snakes; they'd charge a man without provocation and rip him up, and sports from Chattanooga came up in November and hunted them with Platt hounds. The Platt hounds were a strain of Airedale.

One of these boars had killed a man in the Unaka Mountains around Christmastime, a fine hunter who'd had two of these Platt hounds; the hunter had got into a corner, apparently, and the boar had got him and one of the hounds. Nobody knew where the other hound had gone. It never came home, and nobody found it anywhere.

Jake had been interested in the story because he'd never known before that boars were in the state, and because they awakened in him the memories of his most devastating boyhood fear. His grandfather, a genial, bearded old wood carver from the Harz Mountains, had pictured them as more dangerous than tigers—great four-hundred-pound brutes with six-inch tusks, lying malignantly in wait for hunters in the gloomy Prussian forests, peering out of the shadows with their evil little pig eyes.

The involuntary shiver accompanying these youthful imaginings came back to him again as he recalled the lawyer's talk. Then the horse stopped abruptly, with a snort, almost pitching Jake over its head.

He clawed his way back into the saddle, staring between the horse's erect ears. An animal had emerged from the shadows about forty feet ahead and stood facing him. He had been so preoccupied with boars that he thought for an instant he was looking at one of them.

The hair on his neck stirred, and his mind searched frantically for a way of getting the horse off the trail if it charged. Then he saw that it wasn't a boar, but a dog. He kicked the horse and moved forward. The dog looked like an Airedale; it had a rough tan-and-black coat. It stood in the path, watching quietly, neither friendly nor unfriendly, with such a withdrawn, self-sufficient quality about it that Jake's curiosity was aroused; for no dog would be on that lonely mountain unless it was lost, and lost dogs were usually pathetically glad to see anyone.

"Hello!" Jake said, and grinned. He had a disarming grin that bunched his cheeks and crinkled the corners of his eyes. "Hello, fellow!"

The dog wagged its tail slightly, but made no advances. He slid off the horse, and, walking to it, ran his square, strong fingers along its spine and around the bases of its ears. It was very thin; the rough coat was stretched over the ribs, but the muscles were hard and tight. It accepted the handling as it had accepted his greeting, undemonstratively. Jake's fingers caught in the thin collar concealed by the rough coat, and he turned it until the brass plate came up. The plate was engraved:

ROUSE
A. YANCY
ELM MILLS
TENN.

Jake straightened up quickly and stared at the dog. All his memories of Yancy came back to him again, bringing a sense of protest, a poignant sense of loss; for he realized instantly that this was the dog the lawyer had talked about, the dog that had vanished after its master had been killed by the boar. It was as if something fine, something very necessary to him, had suddenly gone out of his life. It was almost impossible for him to believe. Yancy was invincible; the boar must have caught him unaware; and as this thought came into Jake's mind he began to hate the boar. He had never had cause to hate an animal before.

Confused by this new emotion, he continued to stare at the dog; and as he stared at it wonder came into his mind. What was it doing here, fifty miles from the scene of Yancy's death, hard miles in a mountainous country where some of the peaks ran up over five thousand feet? The fight had occurred six months ago. Where had the dog sheltered during the bitter mountain winter? Was it so grieved by Yancy's death that it had become a wanderer, mourning for him? That it had traveled widely was evident from its muscles; that it had managed to survive at all was an unbelievable thing.

Jake bent over it with closer attention. There was a long scar, nearly healed over, along its left side. The boar must have done that, must have scored with those terrible six-inch tusks.

Thinking of its loyalty and its loneliness, feeling his own sense of loss, Jake wanted the dog. He wanted it more than the three he had at home: Bella, the Virginia shepherd, or the two coon hounds, Music and Plunger. They were good dogs, but not one of them could have gone on in loneliness and privation as this dog had done; not one of them was connected with the memories this dog invoked. He'd take it home. "Rouse!" he said. "Rouse!"

The dog raised its head quickly and looked at him, its ear pricked. Its eyes were attentive and questioning, but it seemed to look beyond him, waiting, as though expecting the familiar syllable to be spoken by another voice. Jake mounted, walked the horse a few steps, and turned. Rouse hadn't moved. He was standing beside the trail, looking after Jake, waiting and attentive.

"Rouse" Jake called. "Rouse!"

The dog's docked tail wagged slightly. For a moment he stood there, a lonely figure against the thicket's dark shadows, then turned and trotted from the trail. Jake called his name again, urgently, then whistled, but he didn't reappear. Far off in the undergrowth a twig cracked, and then silence fell; regretfully, Jake rode on.

In the deep, narrow little valley where Jake's farm lay, things fell back into their accustomed routine. The hired man, Rufe—a lanky, drawling mountain man, had carried things on and there was no back work to catch up. Jake worked the corn and the vegetable patches with Rufe, sent Bella out to drive in the two cows at milking time, and spent the short evenings reading and carving little figures before the fire with the three dogs around him. Isolated as he was, he had a lonely, quiet life, which suited him; he had a little money, kept his place neatly, and fared better than the few families round about. He would have been happy if he hadn't encountered Rouse.

The remembrance of the dog standing lonely and waiting in the trail stayed with him, that and the sense of loss over Yancy's death. Yancy became real to him once more; and, thinking so much of Yancy, of the empty place left by Yancy's death, Jake wanted the dog increasingly. It would have been a link with the past, and he was sure it had wanted to come with him. The expression of its eyes indicated plainly that it knew well enough what it was giving up.

He knew the dog liked him; they all liked him. They seemed to understand at once the kindliness of his square strong hands and of his sentimental German heart, to accept him without reservations. He fulfilled their need of warmth and affection, the ancient heritage of their domesticity. No dog had ever refused to follow him before. It was, in a way, an indication of their softness, an indication that their need of affection was the greatest thing in their lives. The fact that Rouse was not bound by this, that he had set out upon a lonely and sorrowful odyssey, gave him a striking individuality and set him apart, made him a dog worthy of Yancy.

Jake couldn't get the dog out of his mind. He would sit thinking about him, staring into the fire with his pipe or a half-finished carving in his hand, until the outraged Bella would get up from her rug and thrust her head into his lap.

There came an afternoon when Jake, busy in his little shop behind the barn, looked up and realized that dusk was beginning to fall. He wondered why Bella wasn't back; for he had sent her after the cows and she was always back before the light began to fail, barking in the yard to let them know the cows were ready to be milked.

He put the chisel back into the rack and went outside. The cows were standing uneasily in the yard, but Bella was nowhere in sight. For the first time Jake thought of the boar. A sudden, tense uneasiness took hold of him, and he ran into the house. Rufe, with the two hounds near him, was washing in the kitchen and raised his dripping face questioningly.

"Bella," Jake said. "Where's Bella?"

"I ain't seen her," Rufe said. "Likely—"

Jake, grabbing the rifle from the corner, interrupted him. "Keep the hounds here," he said, and jamming a cartridge into the rifle ran out. He could hear the hounds' sudden uproar of excitement as he ran.

The cows trotted off a few yards and stared stupidly at him as he went past them; he finally pulled up, panting, at the edge of the pasture. It was a triangular piece of land, narrowing before him to its apex between the steep sides of the ridge, broken by clumps of willow and birch. Shadows were deepening over it; but off to the left, among the darkening tangle, his eye caught a faint gleam of white.

"Bella!" he shouted. "Bella!"

The white spot didn't move. But before the echo of his voice died out, the boar moved in the cover and vanished again, a great dark beast frosted with gray, with a head nearly as large as its body. The tusks gleamed for an instant in the gloom and then it was gone.

He made a step to go after it, but something inside him tightened up and stopped him. It was dark in there, dark and thick; in the darkness the brute that had been too much for Yancy waited. The memories of his grandfather's tales moved obscurely in his mind, and his legs refused to move. He couldn't go on. He stood waiting for the boar to go away, knowing what he would find. Bella had been a splendid bitch of a local breed, affectionate and trustworthy, too unsuspicious and accustomed to the ways of domestic cattle and swine for the sudden, unexpected and slashing ferocity of the boar.

He went back to the house and picked up the old hooked rug on which she had slept. Rufe put the hounds in the kitchen and went back with him without speaking. In silence they wrapped Bella's body in the rug and buried her where the boar had killed her.

It was dark when they returned to the barn and got the cows milked and bedded down, and the hounds had fallen quiet. They didn't talk about it even then. Rufe muttered a subdued "Night," and went to bed early. Jake spent the evening before the fire; once or twice he looked up from it to see where Bella was.

Slow rage began to burn within him. He finally went to bed, but he couldn't sleep; as he tossed about, his rage increased. The hate he had felt for the boar upon learning of Yancy's death had been an abstract emotion, for hate was alien to him; further, he had been preoccupied with thoughts of Yancy and Rouse. Now that the boar had appeared, however, the rage was abstract no longer, and Bella's death had intensified it.

He clenched his fists beneath the blankets, wanting to kill the boar, to do away with it for its senseless ferocity in taking Yancy and Bella away from him. He recalled his unwillingness at the pasture's edge, but as his rage increased he excused himself for it. It would have been foolhardy, he thought, to go into the dark thicket. Daylight was the time to deal with a brute like that, and in the morning he'd deal with it. Under this determination something very like fear lurked, but he had worked himself past the point of seeing it.

Early in the morning Rufe found him making sandwiches by lamplight. Rufe, as was his custom, asked no questions; but he stood by, so obviously expecting an explanation that Jake finally said: "It was a boar killed Bella. I'm going after it."

"A boah?" Rufe asked, and rubbed his long chin. "I ain't seen nary a boah evah, but I heah tell they's pow'ful mean. I reckon I'll go along."

Jake shook his dark head. "No," he said, "you stay here."

"Likely you'll need help. I reckon I'll go."

"No," Jake said. Although he tried to control his voice it took a faint edge of irritation.

Rufe gave in. "Sure," he said. "Only don't you mess with no rifle. You take the gun. Likely you'll come up with him in a thick place, where the shootin's close and quick. You mind out, Jake. You mind out. I ain't likin' no boahs."

Jake agreed, dismissed him to his work, locked the hounds in the kitchen, and started out. He went first to the pasture, back into the thickets where the boar had been. Its tracks were easily followed for a way, but he lost them on higher ground. Then he recalled his grandfather saying that boars in the old country usually hid in the daytime and moved about at dusk and dawn. After that, he stayed close to thicker cover, along the streams and near boggy places.

He hunted slowly and carefully, in a cold rage. He was always in the shadows, and after a while it became touchy work. His imagination began to overcome his rage, and by noon his nerves were playing him tricks. For each gloomy thicket he drew blank the tension increased. The realization that the boar had been too much for Yancy came closer all the time; the expectation built up that the next thicket would bring the boar down on him, in a place too thick to swing the gun.

It was nearly noon by the sun when he decided to quit. He had worked into another narrow little valley, and it was swampy and thick; he didn't like the look of it from the first, but he went into it. The shadows fell cool and deep, and when a rabbit burst from its squat with a great rattle of twigs his heart leaped up with it. He hesitated, then decided to go to the end of the thicket. The shadows grew more secretive and menacing.

He could never remember, afterward, the start of the boar's charge. One moment was held by brooding silence; the next filled the world with crashing pandemonium. The gun leaped up, caught a branch and was torn from his hands. The next instant the black bulk was upon him. Its size was far beyond his expectations, and it moved with unbelievable speed.

He had one swift impression of the great ugly head with its gleaming tusks, and leaped sideways. There was a blow; a mighty hand to which his weight was nothing, seemed to catch at his leg, spin him into the air, and hurl him down. He scrambled up desperately, caught a limb, and swung himself clear as the boar charged again. It raged about below as he pulled his legs up and flattened on a limb, making short, vicious rushes, gashing great splinters from the trunk, squealing and gnashing jaws slobbered with foam.

In quickness and malevolent power it was even worse than his grandfather had claimed; it was truly a devil come out of his boyhood. It held him there for nearly an hour, charging about and looking wickedly up at him, then went reluctantly off. Only then did he discover that one leg of his heavy corduroys had been cleanly slit from cuff to knee and the skin of his leg beneath it left with a long red welt.

An uncontrollable nervous trembling seized him as he stared at it. The charge had been a near thing, a moment of pure, blind terror, and he knew he couldn't face another one. It wasn't the fear of death that brought him to this. He had faced death calmly several times; there was plenty of courage in his stocky body. It was a fear of the boar, an uncontrollable and violent revulsion of his nerves latent in him since boyhood, an irresistible revolt against a certain object, just as another man's nerves would have revolted against a snake. He realized that his nerves and not his mind had tricked him, that he had been beaten before he went into the thicket. He had let the killer of Yancy and Bella escape; but the thing that stabbed him was his failure to dominate himself. The code he had built upon Yancy had failed, and in failing he had let Yancy down. Sentimental in most things, he was not sentimental in this; there was a very bitter taste in his mouth.

Now that his fear was fully revealed, Jake didn't try to justify it again. There was too much forthright honesty in him for that. It was there and he couldn't escape it; neither could he bear to live with it. He considered endless expedients for killing the boar, but could hit upon nothing practical. He fretted over it until his mind, as a defense measure, swung him into the belief that the boar had moved on and wouldn't come to the farm again, that it was beyond his reach in the wilderness surrounding him.

This was a poor escape and he half realized it; he was silent and unhappy; for three days he worked alone, with the hounds near him and the rifle handy, and his bitterness at himself mounted. On the third afternoon he was walking from the barn to the house, the hounds beside him, when they suddenly leaped, growling, toward the porch. He looked up, yelling at them, to see Rouse standing by the steps. He was too surprised to yell again.

Rouse stood still, and the hounds bore down on him. He was an interloper, a stranger, and the hounds intended to drive him off. They made for him together, and he didn't move until they were almost upon him. By that time Jake had gathered his wits sufficiently to yell again. He wanted Rouse desperately, and he thought that Rouse, like most dogs so attacked in a strange place, would turn tail and be lost to him. He yelled with all the strength of his lungs, but it was too late to stop the hounds. They leaped in; but instead of running, Rouse side-stepped with flashing quickness, rolled Plunger over by a shoulder blow, and slashed Music.

While Jake ran for them the fight practically settled itself. Rouse was everywhere at once, slashing them both, bounding between them with a swift and expert coolness that left them snapping empty air. They were seasoned fighters, but by the time Jake ran up they'd had enough and were ready to be called off. He put them into the house, came out again, sat down on the step, and called Rouse to him.

Rouse came and stood before him quietly, friendly but withdrawn, accepting the hands that stroked his head. Lonely and depressed, Jake at first stroked him without thought, soothed by the dog's presence and association with Yancy. But, as the rhythmic play of his fingers continued, a sort of confidence seemed to enter them from the clean, hard skull, a feeling that the dog would help him vanquish his fear. As this hope was born in Jake he began to talk to the dog softly and ingratiatingly; his hands, shrewd in their knowledge of nerve centers, played more widely over the dog in an effort to bind it to him.

As he rubbed the harsh coat he noticed the scar again. It was all but healed; and as he looked at it he realized that it had healed more during the short time since he had seen the dog than it had during the entire winter. He puzzled over that for a moment. Suddenly it came to him: Rouse hadn't got the scar when Yancy died. He had got it after that, much later. Rouse's wanderings weren't from grief, but had a grim purpose. Ever since Yancy's death Rouse had trailed the boar, forever seeking and fighting it, hounding it implacably, determined to run it down.

Jake stopped running and stared at the dog, his imagination caught by the spirit of Nemesis in the thin, iron-muscled body. In his mind's eye he saw Rouse wandering through the freezing cold and snow of winter, the fogs and raw winds of spring, lonely and starving, blind to suffering and fear, terribly outclassed by the boar, but never giving in. The odds were all against him, yet he had kept on fighting a desperate guerrilla warfare of ambush and swift attack and flight. Again and again it had happened: the dash in the shadows, the squealing, murderous charge, the frantic work.

Such iron courage shamed him by making him realize his own evasions, but it brought him hope as well; hope that the dog's example, like Yancy's so long ago, would aid him in defeating his traitorous nerves. The saving warmth of this hope leaped up in him; he ran into the house, returned with a heaping plate of meat, and watched Rouse eat. When the dog had finished, he called it into the house. It entered quietly and stayed near him; the hounds bristled, but kept their distance.

Rufe came in and accepted Rouse as he had accepted the first hunt for the boar; he knew Jake would tell the whole story when he felt like it. Jake talked to Rouse while the supper was cooked and eaten; when he lighted the fire and sat down before it Rouse lay down on the small rug before the hearth, watching him for a while, and went to sleep. He slept profoundly; but even in sleep he remained a little remote, a visitor who appreciated hospitality, but withheld allegiance.

Jake smoked and watched him, more at peace than he had been for days, the hope warm within him. He was sure that now he had Rouse inside, warmed and fed and comfortable, he would be able to keep him. When he was sure of the dog they could start out together. The fire died down and he got up; Rouse got up, too, and going to the door scratched upon it.

"No," Jake said. "You'd better stay inside tonight."

Rouse whined from the door, and Jake walked over to him. Outside, the moon was full; the barn and the little valley were overlaid with calm silver, and beyond them the ridge thrust up sharp and black into the luminous sky. Rouse whined and thrust an ingratiating moist nose into his hand.

"No, no, old fellow," Jake said. "I need you here." He went into the bedroom. Rouse followed, moving restlessly about, and finally Jake took him into the living room. "Lie down," he said. Rouse went to the hearthrug, but remained standing as Jake closed the bedroom door.

Jake got into bed. He heard Rouse come to his door and whine once more. "Go to bed, Rouse," he said, quietly and kindly.

The dog moved about for a short while; then there

was the quick patter of feet and a crash. The hounds bayed; Jake jumped out of bed and ran into the living room. Rouse wasn't there, and the window overlooking the porch was broken. Jake ran to the door and pulled it open, but Rouse had gone.

Jake came back into the living room and kicked up the fire. He didn't sit down. He rested one hand on the mantel he'd carved himself, and stood perfectly still, high-lighted softly by the flames. For a while there was only one thought in his head: That Rouse, with the strange prescience of animals had sensed the fear in him, had realized that if he stayed Jake would gradually give up the determination to go after the boar. This thought may have been fantastic or it may have been true; Jake was in no emotional state to analyze it; the saving thing was that it brought to him a shame more unbearable than his fear.

His mind became full of pictures of Rouse and Rouse's courageous and hopeless struggles with the boar. And beneath all this, he knew the boar would be back; some day it would come out of the shadows to attack the cows or Rufe or himself. He stood there with his belly going hollow and cold within him, and knew that he would have to face the boar alone.

Once more Rufe entered the lamplit kitchen as he was making up his pack, and stood silently by. He looked up. Rufe's eyes were on him solemnly; Rufe's long face expressed concern. Jake, tired by the emotions of the night, and apprehensive, suddenly felt grateful to him for his silent and unobtrusive sympathy. "I'm going after him again, Rufe," he said. "I can't let him run me off my own place."

Rufe nodded. "I figgered you was studyin' on it," he said. "I reckon this time I ain't stayin' heah."

"Yes," Jake said. "I'd like you to stay here this

time too."

Rufe's long jaw set. "It's right discomfortable stayin' heah. I ain't such a weaklin' in a scuffle."

"You're a good man anywhere," Jake said, "but I have to settle this myself." He forestalled Rufe's protest. "Have you ever been afraid of anything, Rufe?"

"I reckon," Rufe said. "Back to home, I was skeert of Lije Harkness. He pestered me, and I was pow'ful skeert of him. I was always studyin' to git my kin and tromple him."

"And what did you do?"

Rufe grinned sheepishly. "Come a day, I rose and trompled him myself. I was too skeert not to tromple him."

"It's the same thing," Jake said. His brown eyes pleaded for Rufe to make it easier. "You see why you can't go."

Rufe considered, long and heavily. "I reckon," he said, then added hopefully: "Only, this hawg ain't no Harkness. Harknesses come clean out in the open when they lay for you." He glanced at Jake to see if this ingenious bypath should be followed up, and saw that it shouldn't. "Well," he said with resignation, "I got work outside. I shore wish you luck, Jake. You git that dawg, can you find him."

Jake nodded; they shook hands without speaking again, their hands gripping hard, and Rufe went out. As Jake pulled the straps tight on his pack, Music, unable to keep still longer, came wiggling over to him.

"You can go," Jake said. "You've got to go this time. And maybe you won't come back. Lie down now."

Music returned to his place. Jake got into his denim coat, eased the pack onto his back, and took a long look around the familiar room. He got the gun and a pocketfull of buckshot shells, tied Music to his belt will a ten-foot length of cord, picked up the rug on which Rouse had slept, and went outside. The hounds scrambled excitedly about, but he called them and made them sniff the rug.

"Find dog!" he ordered. "Find dog!" The hounds lost some of their enthusiasm and looked at him unhappily. He knew he would have trouble holding them to Rouse's scent, but it could be done. "Find dog!" he ordered again.

They went out past the barn and through the pasture, then began to work up the ridge. At first Jake was very jumpy, but as the outlines of leaves overhead strengthened against the paling sky and the details of rocks and deadfall timber emerged from the general monotone of the ground a sort of detachment came on him. There was a penetrating chill in the air, and the woods were dripping wet; Music constantly entangled his rope in the underbrush, and Plunger worked too far ahead and had to be called in frequently.

Jake was afraid to let Music off the rope for fear both hounds would get too far ahead and be lost; he endured the tugging and entanglements patiently. By the time the sun was up his detachment had deepened into a sort of numbness that went all through him and even immobilized thought. Only his nerves were alive.

By early afternoon his muscles were aching. He had been climbing stiff ridges or sliding down them since sunrise, with his nerves at an increasing tensity, and the constant pull of Music at his belt hadn't helped. The hounds were tiring too; it was increasingly difficult to control them. But he went on, and presently came out into a small glade with a tumbling stream on the edge of it.

The grass had been torn up and the bushes flattened, and as Jake searched around he found a few spots of dried blood on a gray rock and the footprints of both dog and boar. His hands began to tremble, and he endeavored to get the hounds on Rouse's scent. Their hackles rose as they sniffed about, but otherwise they refused to take any interest. They'd had enough of it; they looked at him mournfully, sat down, and ran their tongues out.

Jake cursed them wanly and set out again. The cold hollowness returned to his belly, and suddenly, against the late afternoon stillness of the woods in which even the leaves hung motionless, his heart began to pound in his ears.

They came to another opening, a parklike place surrounded by small maples. Plunger was trotting twenty feet ahead when suddenly he stiffened and snarled. There was a crash of underbrush, and Jake didn't have time for fear, for any conscious thought whatever. The boar burst out of the maples and came for him, head down, like a black projectile. Plunger leaped aside, and the boar, turning with the sudden, lunging quickness of all swine, made for Music. Jake fired, Music dodged with a yank on the cord that ruined his aim, and the boar went between them, cutting the cord.

The boar wheeled and came for Jake. Both hounds closed in on it, and Plunger was tossed into the air. Jake fired the other barrel. The boar fell forward and leaped up again. It started to squeal. Music fastened on its hind leg, but it whirled and tossed Music, too, and came again for Jake.

Although Jake might have had time to reload the gun, he never thought of it. He forgot the gun entirely. For an instant he stood there, frozen, staring at the squealing boar. He saw in violent motion the heavy, bristled shoulders and the gleaming tusks, the evil little eyes, and the terror of it rushed over him.

The overwhelming urge to avoid it, the nerves' blind panic, held him powerless; and as he stared, something happened to his sense of time. The swift action became slowed and prolonged, like the action in a dream. There was a long moment when his courage went out to meet the boar, unfaltering and bright, and he recognized the courage and was glad of it.

And then, from beyond his field of vision, Rouse appeared and tore the boar's hindquarters The boar squealed on a higher note; he saw it turn with an upward sweep of the tusks, but Rouse leaped clear as a salmon leaps clear of a wave. Twisting and beautifully coordinated, he side-stepped another charge and sank his teeth in the boar and leaped aside. But he didn't leap away; he closed once more and the boar tossed him, but even then he didn't retreat. He twisted in the air and recovered his balance, feinted and attacked; then Jake knew that the old guerrilla tactics were done with. Rouse had heard the gun; he knew that Jake was somewhere near and counted on him and would fight until he came.

Safe now to climb a maple and escape, Jake knew what the finish would be. Only one finish was possible unless he intervened; and foreseeing the death of the dog because it knew only Yancy's courage, he was lifted above the spell that his nerves had imposed upon his mind. His mind commanded once more. He jammed two shells into the gun, and with the loathing and terror of the boar rising in him like a physical sickness he ran toward it.

Rouse spun into the air, and the boar back-stepped, squealing, throwing its head up to rend him as he fell. The bloody foam of its jaws was flung over Jake, and its mad eyes rolled toward him; against the defeated and intolerable protest of his nerves he ran closer to it and fired both barrels into its head. Its legs collapsed and it fell. Rouse dropped a short distance away, whipped about and fastened upon it. But it never moved again, and Rouse relinquished his hold and stood looking at Jake.

Jake stared back at him. The hounds came up, but Jake was only dimly aware of them. He knew that he was worthy of Yancy at last, that the code he had built upon Yancy was safe forever, and a great feeling of triumph was born in him.

"Rouse!" he said. "Rouse!"

The dog looked once more at his dead enemy, then came toward Jake. His side was raked and bleeding and he limped, but his eyes had lost entirely their expression of questioning and remoteness.

Jake bent down, his hands reaching out to rub the harsh coat along the spine, but Rouse forestalled him. He put his head on Jake's lowered shoulder and licked Jake's ear with a quick, warm urgency. They stayed that way for a moment, and when Jake straightened up and walked away from the dead boar Rouse walked beside him, his head under Jake's hand.

He knows, Jake thought, he's sure now. Maybe, before, he could feel that I was afraid. That's over, and he'll never go away again. And Yancy knows, too; he's Yancy's and mine.

His fingers touched the clean, narrow terrier skull, and the sense of triumph came over him more keenly than before.